LINUX FOR BEGINNERS

The easy beginner's guide to introduce and use Linux operating system. How to make an easy installation, configuration, learn basics commands, fundamentals and technical overview.

[Matthew Python]

1

Legal & Disclaimer

The information contained in this book and its contents is not designed to replace or take the place of any form of medical or professional advice; and is not meant to replace the need for independent medical, financial, legal or other professional advice or services, as may be required. The content and information in this book has been provided for educational and entertainment purposes only.

The content and information contained in this book has been compiled from sources deemed reliable, and it is accurate to the best of the Author's knowledge, information and belief. However, the Author cannot guarantee its accuracy and validity and cannot be held liable for any errors and/or omissions. Further, changes are periodically made to this book as and when needed. Where appropriate and/or necessary, you must consult a professional (including but not limited to your doctor, attorney, financial advisor or such other professional advisor) before using any of the suggested remedies, techniques, or information in this book.

Upon using the contents and information contained in this book, you agree to hold harmless the Author from and against any damages, costs, and expenses, including

Table of Contents

5

Introduction

Linux is the predecessor of the UNIX operating system that took the computer industry by storm in its initial days. The kernel that is the heart of Linux is named after its creator Linux Torvalds. Linux operating system at present is the most used open-source operating system now on the planet.

To put things straight learning Linux is one of the most essential skills in today's competitive world. Linux runs on almost all databases and web environments. High-level enterprises use Linux to maintain their networks and databases. Android, one of the most famous operating system also runs on the Linux Kernel. Almost every programmer at one point in his professional life prefers Linux to complete tasks.

Apart from its numerous advantages Linux also offers stable and smooth performance than windows. This book is a comprehensive beginner's introduction to Linux along with a lot of layman examples and shell codes.

What is Linux?

Linux is an operating system that runs with the help of kernel surrounded by applications and extensions that run with the help of it. Every application is in some way connected to the kernel. To explain in simple terms every part of the system uses the Linux kernel to run efficiently. Hardware and network communications both need kernel support to function efficiently. Many misunderstand that the Linux kernel is an operating system but it is just a component of a complete operating system.

Different Linux distro publishers like Red hat, Debian, Arch adopts the functionalities that kernel provides and add more tools, libraries to build a complete operating system. Every Linux distro publisher uses certain guidelines and uses the kernel to customize their operating system. For example, Parrot Linux a hacking operating system provides different pen-testing tools for its users in the distro when they install.

Why is Linux Essential in Today's world?

First of all, Linux is a must for programmers and hackers as it is much more reliable and robust. As it is cheap to maintain almost 50% of the intranet and internet applications use Linux as a primary operating system. Apache software that runs on Linux is primarily used in server-based applications.

Linux also supports a lot of hardware systems and needs less hardware to function. For this reason, a lot of small industries are looking forward to starting their business with the help of Linux based systems. Linux based systems are also used in future technologies such as Artificial Intelligence, Data Science, Big Data, Data Analytics, Augmented Reality and Virtual Reality.

What did we cover in this book?

This book is a complete Layman's introduction for beginners. In the beginning, we will introduce Linux and its history in detail. As we proceed further, we will learn about installation procedures and SSH clients in detail. This book also provides a section where we will discuss

Linux commands in detail. Different Linux core concepts such as process management, File management will be explained in detail. The last section of this book will deal with advanced shell programming and Log analysis that are necessary for an efficient Linux scientist.

How to utilize this book perfectly?

This book provides both concepts and programming code whenever necessary in detail. To utilize this book perfectly practice the concepts and implement them in your own projects. This becomes can also be used as a quick reference.

Thanks for downloading this book. Let us start exploring the beautiful and exciting world of Linux. Let us go!

Chapter 1: What is Linux?

With the advent of technology, the world has rapidly developed. Computers have made a lot of things easier and are an obvious choice for doing both automated and complex tasks. Computers in the first generation used a lot of resources and had occupied large rooms to store mere kilobytes of information. In the past computers that do basic mathematical operations are only available for commercial and military purposes and are in no way available for the general public.

Due to this operating system such as Minix are often hugely priced and are often not affordable. However, with the entrance of Macintosh and Windows things got changed rapidly and households soon got used to computers. Even these revolutionary operating systems are commercialized and their source code still remains confidential.

Then on one fine day creation of Linux kernel system has changed the scope of the open-source system. Now, after 25 years Linux is the most preferred operating system by all experts, database professionals, penetration testers and developers with hundreds of Linux distributions available in both free and commercial licenses.

This chapter on a whole will give you a complete layman's introduction to the operating system, Open source revolution, Unix operating systems, A bit of Linux history and information about some of the most basic and popular Linux distributions available now. Let us start!

What is an Operating system?

The operating system acts as a communication between humans and computers to makes things easier. Humans use linguistic languages to communicate among themselves whereas Computers use machine Languages to communicate with their resources and to take instructions.

It is not practically possible to input instructions in binary languages by humans because it takes a lot of time and skill. This is the sole reason why programmers started to develop an interface that acts as a medium between humans and computers. As time progressed programmers understood the potential of this invention and started to integrate with a lot of useful operations such as Graphical user interface, Memory management, Process Management, Advanced security to get combined into an operating system.

The most popular Operating system is windows and often shares the commercial market with Mac. Linux is also an operating system but is available for anyone for free and anyone can modify the kernel to create their own Linux distributions for both personal and commercial purposes. This special category of the operating system is called as Open-sourced operating systems. In the next section, we will go through a thorough explanation about open source and discuss its impacts and challenges.

What is an Open Source?

The open source systems and software are designed on a principal motto to share source code file along with the software or operating system. When the desired user gets hands on the open-source system he is completely allowed to change the source code file to include new features or integrate them into hardware systems to develop into derivative products.

Linux is completely an open-source system and is one of the important reasons for its rapid increase among users. Linux user base is often occupied by technical experts, programmers, and hackers. However, with the development of Linux distributions such as Ubuntu, Centos Linux has occupied a good share among normal users too.

What are the objectives of open source systems?

1) Low risk

Open-source systems are often not prone to bankruptcy as they are maintained not by individuals but by a group of enthusiastic and considerate programmers using git.

2) High quality

Open source programming software is often of high quality as different contributors try to add new features and fix the bugs as soon as they find it. Commercial operating systems such as Windows are often slow to fix the bugs and this can sometimes result in attacks from hackers using an exploit. A famous example includes Ransom ware Worm which utilized a bug in the windows to exploit thousands of computers.

3) Low cost

Open-source systems are mostly developed by contributors who are willing to work on a project to increase their expertise and skills. These programmers don't use development as a source of income but to make things better for everyone involved.

4) Different License Agreements

Open-source systems also provide the usage of different licenses according to the creator's decision. If you are looking forward to contributing to the open-source revolution it is recommended to learn about different Licenses such as GPL, BSD, Apache, MPL, MIT in detail.

A brief history of Linux

In the early 1970s which is considered as a renaissance period for computers, there are traces of open source development. UNIX is one of the most favorite enterprises that has been used by programmers to develop software that can be freely distributed anywhere. However, the open-source community was devastated when UNIX decided to commercialize all of its integrated resources making it hard for the open-source community to effectively develop applications.

Several companies tried to make things normal but only things got better when Richard Stallman in 1984 started the GNU open-source program. It was followed by the release of the GCC compiler which made programmers create their own programs for the environment. These resources helped programmers to create quite innovative applications.

Out of all of them, in 1991 a project created by a young student from Helsinki University started to top the charts in the community. It is primarily an operating system that consists of a kernel that consists of different libraries which can be used to integrate and develop third party applications and distributions. This young student, Linux Torvalds overwhelmed by the response started taking the project seriously and entered a full swing of development. This project is called "Linux".

By 1994, Linux has boomed exponentially in both popularity and user base. In the same year, a programmer named Bob Young integrated different libraries to the kernel and released his own commercial distribution known as Red Hat Linux to enterprises. With the success of Red Hat, people understood the advantages of Linux based systems and started to integrate it into different technical systems. Linux Torvalds still operates the kernel from his home to date with the help of hundreds of thousands of enthusiastic programmers contributing from all over the world.

In 2019, Linux occupies a 15% share of the technical landscape and consists of hundreds of Linux distributions that can be used for different purposes. For example, Kali

Linux is a Linux distribution that is solely developed for hackers.

How is Linux different from the windows?

Even though windows occupy the major share in the market Linux is considered best among all the operating systems due to its robust performance, simple interfaces, and advanced security mechanisms. In this section, we will look at all the features that help Linux occupy the top tier of operating systems.

a) Open-source

As discussed before Linux is one of the few operating systems that license all of its source code to be used by anyone. For enthusiastic people who are technically sound enough to change the source code according to their requirements can find Linux useful.

b) Can be used anywhere

As technology prospered hardware technology too prospered making lower-end systems unsupportive for latest windows versions. However, with Linux, you can find different lightweight distros to equip with your lower end personal computers. Android, a famous mobile operating system also runs on the Linux kernel. Linux also can be used to be integrated into embedded systems such as Arduino. Basically, Linux can be used from a mobile phone to an automobile making it one of the few operating systems that provide this volatility.

c) A dream place for programmers

Programmers often rely on Linux systems to debug, program and test their source code. Linux platform various integrated development environments for almost all programming languages available. Advanced data science and artificial intelligence projects often rely on Linux systems to collaborate and organize their resources. Programmers can also depend on the Windows system to develop applications but the fast processing speed of Linux results in fast debugging and deployment of software.

d) Better customization

Windows and Mac restrict users to follow their basic user interface for different reasons. Users who are looking forward to customizing their systems need to install third-party software which is often costly. For geeks who love beautiful interfaces, Linux is the best option as it offers hundreds of inbuilt themes and comes in different customizable environments such as KDE and GNOME.

e) Advanced update system

Linux offers a fast and reliable way to update the operating system. Windows and Mac often provide updates a considerable time even after finding bugs due to fewer contributors maintaining the enterprise systems. Linux, on the other hand, provides updates for its users in very little time due to the fast development of the resources. Different Linux distributions use different pre-made update installers and can be customized using different filters according to the user choice.

f) Awesome terminal

Everyone who is a little geeky will understand how buggy Microsoft's command prompt is. The terminal in Linux is a pathway to operate different systems that are operated by the kernel. You can control the whole system using commands that are pre-built and customized. You can even edit system files using the Linux terminal whereas Windows often restricts users with very basic usage of command prompt.

g) High-level security

Linux offers high-level security with its anonymity features. Some Linux distros even provide TOR proxy chains along with the system. It is often tough for hackers to manipulate Linux systems as they are designed to defend attacks. Windows, on the other hand, is often prone to attacks by trojans, viruses, and worms due to its bad defense system. This is the reason why most of the Windows users rely on Antiviruses whereas Linux users need not use them.

h) Support community

Linux has a very generous community of programmers and experienced users willing to help when you are facing problems with the system. Windows also provide a support forum but advanced system errors can only be solved with the help of an expert.

Apart from these advantages, Linux is free and is often easy to install. This rapid advantage of Linux systems has helped them occupy 25% of the market share and is often used by business enterprises to manage their resources. In the next section, we will discuss some of the popular Linux distros that are pioneers now.

Popular Linux Distros

Linux Distros are compelled software packages that are made available as separate operating systems. They are developed using pre-built libraries that Linux offers and integrate them with their compiled applications. Here we will introduce some of the famous Linux distros.

1) Red Hat Enterprise Linux

Red hat Linux is one of the first Linux distributions that has been developed using the Linux kernel. It is now one of the most used enterprise Linux systems in the world. It is known for its strong performance, stability, and detailed statistics. Red hat Linux is often used by enterprises to maintain their databases, Networks and other technical systems. Red hat Linux also provides paid distributions according to the customizations they provide.

2) Manjaro Linux

Manjaro Linux is one of the famous Linux distribution systems that use Arch Linux. Arch Linux is an advanced user integration system that supports faster software installation. Everything is pre-installed unlike other distros and is perfect for beginners. Manjaro also offers great customization options. According to the Internet, Manjaro is the most downloaded Linux Distro in 2018.

3) Ubuntu

Ubuntu is the Linux distro that made Linux easy for normal users. Ubuntu uses the Debian database to sync applications and provide updates automatically. It is lightweight, fast and stable. Ubuntu is often pre-installed in Laptops and computers with fewer specifications for better performance.

4) Linux Mint

Linux Mint has grown into popularity for its easy navigational interfaces. It provides faster updates and can be installed in lower end computers too. It is lightweight and is often free of bugs. Linux mint is one of the popular Linux distros that has a dedicated number of contributors.

With this, we have completed our Basic Introduction to Linux. In the next chapter, we will look at the installation procedures of different Linux systems in detail. Let us go.

29

Chapter 2: Installation of Linux

Installation is a simple procedure if done right. Windows system is often hectic and takes a lot of time where a Linux installation procedure is minimal and often finishes in very little time. However, procedures slightly differ due to a high number of Linux Distros available. In this section, we will try to explain the installation procedure in a way that you can install any Linux operating system both in a virtual machine and by bootable devices. Follow along to know more about it.

Note:

It is always good to have advanced planning before starting the installation procedure. Always learn about the Linux distro you are trying to install in detail. Make a list of necessary things required based on the guide files.

In the below section we will discuss in detail the planning you need to be aware before proceeding with the installation procedure.

a) Always make sure that you satisfy all the system requirements

Different operating systems asks for different requirements to install. Always crosscheck the requirements in the Linux distro website and continue further with the installation procedure if you are sure about the prerequisites. Even with not satisfying requirements, Linux can be installed but you may face several performance issues while using the operating system. So, it is always recommended to use Lightweight Linux distros if you are using older computers with fewer specifications.

b) Should you lose windows?

There are different types of OS installation. You can install the Linux version as a fresh install or you can run both Windows and Linux in the same system. However, a dual boot system can reduce the performance of the operating system. If you are reluctant to use windows then the dual boot is a perfect way. You can also experiment with a virtual machine if you support higher specifications as virtual machines in lower-end computers are buggy.

c) Prepare all of your hardware

Make all your hardware available during the installation procedure. A handful of Linux distros asks you to enter details about hardware devices such as CD-ROM, network card during the installation procedure.

d) Know about the Linux file system

The most important prerequisite to install Linux is to know in detail about Linux file management system. It is mandatory to select the partition information during the installation. Make sure you are thorough about it. We will discuss partition in detail in the further sections of the chapter.

Minimum recommended system

After careful consideration, we are showing you here the minimum system requirement that a Linux operating system needs

1) A good Intel processor

It is recommended to use a system that supports 486 or later Intel microprocessors. AMD and Pentium processors are well recommended for better performance.

2) 1GB RAM

It is recommended to maintain at least 1GB RAM for better performance. As RAM size increases the performance of the Linux system increases exponentially.

3) 20GB free hard disk space

Most of the hard disk space will be occupied by Linux system files. However, it is recommended to maintain at least 20GB free hard disk space to give a seamless and smooth performance.

In the next section, we will discuss in detail about Linux partition systems.

First of all, Linux deals file systems in total contrary to windows. Windows usually represent hard drive using Local disks such as Local disk C, Local disk D, etc...

Whereas Linux represents them as /dev/sda, /dev/sdb... Here a is the first Linux hard drive system and it continues cumulatively.

What is the partition?

Partition is a process in which a hard drive is divided into distinctive pieces to continue with the system installation. There are different partition schemes such as the MBR partitioning scheme. There are different partitioning techniques to be used while installing the Linux system. We will discuss some of them in layman's terms in this section.

As known technically there are three types of partition schemes namely primary, extended and logical.

Usually, a lot of Linux Distribution systems use the following scheme to install.

a) A significant part of the system which is mounted as /root [This consists of system files and are often not editable]

b) A very smaller portion of the drive which is mounted for the RAM. Usually, this partition system is known as swap

c) Normal hard drive partition that can be used to store files. This is usually represented as /home.

You can normally select the partition system sizes during the installation procedures according to your requirements. With this, we have a good understanding of the partitioning and in the next section; we will discuss in detail the installation procedure. We will use Linux Mint as an example Operating system for better understanding.

Installing Linux Mint using bootable media

Linux mint is one of the most popular Linux distros and is well known for its simplicity. We will divide the installation procedure into various steps for better and clear understanding. You can use the same procedure for any Linux distro that you are trying to install.

1) Always research the requirements

As said before it is very important to know about the Distro that you are going to install. Enter the Linux mint website and understand the system requirements and cross-check them. Find out whether your computer is a 64 bit or 32-bit supporting system. This is very important as you need to download the iso file with this option.

How to know if your system is 32 bit or 64 bit?

Enter the control panel in windows and click on the properties tab. You can find the type of system your computer is supporting. You can even look at all of your system specifications using the device information tab. A lot of advanced Linux distros now require higher specifications for using.

2) Download the file

After the initial research, it is now time to download the installer. There are a lot of third-party websites that offer the installation file but it is always recommended to download the installation file from the official website as a lot of installation files are included with Trojans to extract your sensitive information. You can re-verify with

36

the 64bit encrypted key to check whether your installation file is genuine or not.

In the installation download page select the 64 bit or 32-bit system file and save it in your hard disk. You are also forced to select a desktop environment such as XFCE or GNOME during the installation procedure. Desktop environments are classical graphical user interfaces and each has its advantages. Do good research before selecting the graphical interface. We recommend downloading XFCE as it is stable in all computers. You can also try GNOME if your hardware specifications are higher.

3) Making a bootable USB

Linux can be installed using bootable devices. You can burn a CD with the installation file using CD burning software such as NERO to make it a bootable CD. However, nowadays CD drives are becoming extinct and it is recommended to use bootable USB for easier installation.

To make a bootable USB you need to use software such as UNETbootin, Universal USB Installer. There is a lot of software that serves the exact purpose. Below we will discuss the procedure they use to install a bootable installation file in the USB.

a) Usually, you need to select the distribution file and the name of the operating system that you are trying to install.

b) Insert the flash drive (Pen drive) that you are willing to use a bootable USB to the system and the drive appears in the third option. Click on the format drive option for a clean install.

c) Then click start to initiate the procedure. Be careful with the power source as any mishap may result in performing the same procedure all over again.

After the procedure is completed you will get a prompt. Eject the hardware and use it to start the installation procedure.

Even after performing all the steps correctly if your system does not respond to the bootable USB then you need to change settings in the BIOS settings. Every manufacturer uses different BIOS procedures for their systems. Do good research on BIOS settings and disable UEFI settings to initiate the bootable USB mode. Sometimes you may require to disable the secure boot option too for immediate effect.

4) Do a backup

It is important to backup all of your data either in the form of a system file or in the cloud. Every operating system offers simple techniques to back up the data.

5) Installation procedure

After you insert the bootable USB and enter into the boot menu the Linux mint live installation will start. Click on the install now option and the installation starts. We will drive through the steps that appear in the installation procedure now.

Select Language

The first interface will ask you to install your desired language. Normally, English is selected but if you are comfortable with your primary language as a language you can select it.

Install third party addons

In the very next step, you will receive a prompt to install third party music add ons. This is an exclusive music player and codecs that are only available for Linux mint. Select the license option and proceed to the next step in the installation procedure.

Select the type of installation

In this interface, you need to select the type of installation procedure you are willing to proceed with. There are usually three options for this interface which we will explain below.

i) Dual boot installation

If you select this option Linux Mint will be installed along with the Windows operating system you are using. This is often chosen by users due to their adaptability with

Windows. If you are an avid Windows user it makes sense to select this option however Linux performance and stability decrease a bit when the dual boot is selected due to less allocated resources.

ii) Automatic installation

This option completely erases the system memory and does partition too automatically for the user. If you are a beginner and are worried about doing the partition wrong way then select this option to make things easier for you.

iii) Manual installation

This option is recommended only for advanced users as you need to manually enter the partition details here. You need to select the swap memory, system memory partition all by yourself. Read carefully about the partitions systems we have mentioned before to not face any hiccups.

No matter what option you will select Linux mint takes you to the next interface.

Time Zone and keyboard layout

In these interfaces select the time zone you are living in and the keyboard layout you are intending to use. There are a lot of keyboard options for second languages such as Chinese and Japanese.

Enter details about the user

In this interface, you usually need to enter the username and password for the user account. After entering the details and clicking the install button starts the installation procedure.

After some time the operating system gets installed successfully and you can log in into the account using the details entered before.

Troubleshooting errors

If you face any errors ask in a support community or check the troubleshooting guide to solve the most common problems. Changing the BIOS settings is also recommended.

After entering into the system install your desired graphical user interfaces from the settings section. Linux offers a lot of customization abilities for the users. Experiment with the graphical interfaces.

With this, we have completed a detailed description of installing Linux Mint using a bootable medium. In the next section, we will look at the installation procedure using a virtual machine.

Installing Linux Mint in a virtual machine

Virtual machines are usually used to run operating systems in a system. Some of the most popular virtual machine software is virtual box and VMWARE. With the help of this software, you can easily run an operating system from the present operating system itself.

Advantages of virtual box

1) Very easy to use and is easy to switch between both operating systems

2) It is recommended to experiment with a virtual box if you are from a security background. Any viruses or worms will not affect the original operating system.

Disadvantages

1) Requires high specifications such as RAM to give smooth performance

2) Sometimes may result in a sudden halt and can cause frustration.

In the below section we will give a step by step procedure to install Linux Mint on a virtual machine.

1) Install the virtual machine

There are different types of virtual machine software like oracle virtual box and VMWARE. For this book, we will proceed with the Virtual box. Install the software in your operating system and you are all set to use Linux Mint in a virtual machine.

2) Download Virtual box file

Usually, virtual box images are available on the internet for faster access. However, you can even Crete a virtual box file from the ios file available in the Linux mint official website.

3) Create Virtual Machine

Click on the create new button and select all the technical prerequisites such as RAM, memory size and insert the VM file in the next interface. Always select a good memory size for no buggy experience.

4) Proceed with installation

Now continue with the installation procedure as explained before and install any hardware devices if needed. Login with the user name and password.

How to add a Graphical user interface in Linux?

Some Linux distros doesn't automatically give Graphical user interfaces after you install them. Usually some of them just show a black screen with login details. Arch Linux is one of the most famous Linux distros that uses the following pattern.

In this scenario you need to download a supporting display manager for your desktop environment. Different Linux desktop environments such as KDE, XFCE uses

45

different managers for installing Graphical user interfaces. Slim is one of the most downloaded Display managers from the Linux third party servers.

Here is the command to install Slim

sudo apt-get install slim

You can also add Graphical user interfaces for server-based command line interfaces.

After installing display managers all you need to do is look at the commands for starting the system. Usually the command looks in the following template;

sudo service {Display manager name} start

How to add additional software in Linux?

Linux distros usually include a lot of software in the package. However, users often need to install other packages and software's. For suppose Linux distros usually come with Mozilla Firefox and some people may need Google chrome for everyday use.

To install packages Linux uses RPM package mode. RPM packages can be usually downloaded from the websites and included into a directory.

This is the command template that is usually used in Linux distros

sudo apt-get install {package name}

You can use parameters such as update, remove for additional options.

With this we have learned a lot of information on Linux installation procedure. In the next chapters we will discuss about various Linux commands and other Linux features in detail. Follow along!

Chapter 3: Fundamentals of Shell

This chapter first introduces the system kernel and then the relationship and function of terminals, then introduce the 4 advantages of Bash interpreter and makes you learn Linux commands.

This book carefully selects dozens of Linux commands that readers need to learn first, which are related to topics such as system work, system state, working directory, files, directories, packaging, compression, and search. By summarizing the above commands into various subsections in this chapter, you can learn these most basic Linux commands one by one in different categories, laying the groundwork for future learning of more complex commands and services.

Generally speaking, computer hardware is made up of the arithmetic unit, controller, memory, input/output devices, etc. What makes all kinds of hardware devices perform their respective functions and can work together is the system kernel.

The kernel of the Linux system is responsible for completing management tasks such as allocation and scheduling of hardware resources. Thus, the system kernel is too important for the normal operation of the computer, so it is generally not recommended to directly edit the parameters in the kernel, but to let users manage the computer through programs or services developed based on the system call interface to meet the needs of daily work.

It must be affirmed that some graphical tools (such as [Logical Volume Manager (LVM])) in the Linux system is really very useful and greatly reduce the probability of operation errors of operation personnel, which is commendable.

However, many graphical tools are written and are often designed only to complete certain work, lacking the original flexibility and controllability of Linux commands. Moreover, graphical tools consume more system resources than Linux command-line interfaces, so experienced operation and maintenance personnel will not even install graphical interfaces for Linux systems, and they need to connect directly to the Linux system remotely through command line mode when starting operation and maintenance work. I have to say that this is quite efficient.

What is a shell?

Shell is such a command-line tool. Shell (also called terminal or shell) acts as a translator between humans and kernel (hardware). When the user "tells" some commands to the terminal, it will call the corresponding program service to complete some work. The default terminal used by many mainstream Linux systems including the Linux mint system is the Bash (Bourne-Again Shell) interpreter.

The mainstream Linux system chooses Bash, interpreter, as the command line terminal, which has the following four advantages. Readers can appreciate the beauty of the Linux system command line in their future study and production work, and truly love them from their hearts.

1. Use up and down arrow keys to retrieve Linux commands previously executed

2: Command or parameter can be completed with the Tab key only by entering the first few digits

3: Strong batch processing

4. It has practical environment variable function.

Since there is already a useful "translator" like Bash in Linux, it is necessary to learn how to communicate with it. To complete various tasks accurately and efficiently, it is not enough to rely solely on the commands themselves, but also to flexibly adjust the parameters of various commands according to the actual situation.

When you have finished this book and have some working experience, you will surely be able to understand the mysteries of Linux commands. A common format for executing Linux commands is this:

Name of the command [Parameters] [Additional details]

Note that the command name, command parameters and command objects should be separated by the space bar.

Command objects generally refer to the files, directories, users and other resources to be processed.

Command parameters can be in a long format (complete option name) or short format (an abbreviation of a single letter), with-and-as prefixes respectively.

Linux novice cannot execute commands mostly because the parameters are relatively complex, and the parameter values need to be changed according to different commands and requirements. Therefore, if you want to flexibly match various parameters and perform the desired functions, you need a long period of experience.

Examples of Long and Short Formats of Command Parameters

Long format   man --usage

Short format   man -u

In the next section, we will discuss some of the basic Linux commands in detail. Follow along!

Basic Commands

1) echo command

The echo command is used for the value extracted from the terminal output string or variable and is in the format

"echo [enter the string | $ enter the variable]".

For example, the command to output the specified string "This is an example" to the terminal screen is:

[root@sample ~]# echo This is an example

This command will display the following information on the terminal screen:

This is an example

2 date command

The date function can help us to display and set the time or date of the system in the format of "date [option] [+specified format]".

Just enter the parameter beginning with "+" in the powerful date command, and the system time or date can be output according to the specified format. In this way, the command of backing up data can be combined with the time information output in the specified format in daily work.

For example, the packed files are automatically packed into "information-2019-8-2.tar.gz" according to the format of "year-month-day". Users only need to look at the file name to get a general idea of the backup time of each file.

The date command to view the current system time in the default format is as follows:

[root@sample ~]# date

Sat Oct 2 6:21:43 IST 2019

The date command that sets the current time of the system to 9:30 on November 1, 2019, is as follows:

[root@sample ~]# date -s "20191101 9:30:00"

Sat Nov 1 09:30:00 IST 2019

The parameter %j in the date command can be used to see what day of the year today is. This parameter can well distinguish the old and new backup time, that is, the larger the number, the closer it is to the current time.

3. reboot command

The reboot function can help us to restart the system and is formatted as reboot.

Since restarting the computer will involve the management authority of hardware resources, the root administrator can be used by default to restart the computer.

The command is as follows:

[root@sample ~]# reboot

4. power off command

The poweroff function can help us to shut down the system and is in the format poweroff.

This command is the same as the reboot command and involves the management authority of hardware resources. therefore, only root administrators can shut down the computer by default.

The command is as follows:

[root@sample~]# poweroff

5. wget

The wget function can help us to download network files in the terminal in the format of "wget [Parameters] Download Address".

If you don't have any management experience of Linux system, you just need to know the parameters and functions of wget command at present, and then look at the following demonstration experiment.

[root@sample ~]# wget {enter the url address here}

Next, we use the wget command to download recursively all page data and files in the website will be automatically saved to the directory named under the current path after downloading. The command to perform this operation is wget -r -p {enter url and path here}.

6. ps command

The ps function can help us to view the process status in the system in the format of "ps [parameters]".

It is estimated that the reader will be shocked when executing this command for the first time-how can there be so many output values, and how can this be seen?

There are many processes running all the time in Linux system. If they can be managed reasonably, the performance of the system can be optimized. In Linux system, there are five common process states, namely, run, interrupt, non-interrupt, zombie and stop.

As mentioned earlier, command parameters in the Linux system can be divided into long and short formats. Long formats and long formats cannot be merged, and long formats and short formats cannot be merged, but short formats and short formats can be merged, and only one- (minus sign) can be retained after merging. In addition, the ps command can allow the parameter not to be incremented or decremented (-), so it can be written directly as ps aux.

7. top command

The top function can help us to dynamically monitor information such as process activity and system load, and its format is top.

The top command is quite powerful and can dynamically view the operation and maintenance status of the system. It is completely regarded as the "enhanced version of Windows Task Manager" in Linux.

8. pidof command

The pidof function can help us to query the PID value of a specified service process in the format "pidof [Parameters] [Service Name]".

The process number value (PID) of each process is unique, so different processes can be distinguished by PID. For example, you can use the following command to query the PID of ftp service program on your computer:

[root@sample~]# pidof ftp 2323

9. kill command

The kill function can help us to terminate a service process with a specified PID in the format "kill [parameter] [process PID]".

Next, we use the kill command to terminate the process represented by the PID queried by the pidof command above. the command is as follows. The effect of this operation is equivalent to forcibly stopping ftp service.

[root@sample ~]# kill 2323

10 killall command

The killall function can help us to terminate all processes corresponding to a service with a specified name. the format is: "killall [parameter] [service name]".

Generally speaking, the service program of complex software will have multiple processes cooperating to provide services for users. If it is troublesome to end these processes one by one, then the killall command can be used to end all processes carried by a service program in batch.

Let's take httpd service program as an example to end its entire process. Since httpd service program is not installed in system by default, all you need to do at this time is look at the operation process and output results, and then practice after learning the relevant contents.

[root@sample ~]# killall httpd

If we want to stop a command immediately after executing it in the system terminal, we can press Ctrl+C (a shortcut key commonly used in a production environment) at the same time, which will immediately terminate the process of the command.

Or, if some commands output information on the screen continuously during execution, which affects the input of subsequent commands, you can add an ampersand at the end of the command, so that the command will enter the background of the system for execution.

With this we have completed the basic bash skills required for using the Linux system. In the next chapter we will discuss in detail about various other commands that helps you become expert in Linux. As said before always try to check the commands explained here by yourself in your Linux system.

Chapter 4: Basic Linux commands

In the previous chapter, we have learned about some of the very basic Linux commands that are used by Linux administrators and users. In this chapter, we will further try to improve your skills by looking at various distinguished commands based on categories such as system commands, directory commands, and text commands. It is not recommended to remember all these commands by heart but it is good to test by yourselves while reading this book to better understand the importance of these commands. Let us start!

System Commands

System commands are important to learn by a Linux learner for improving the efficiency of the system. This section will help you learn commands that are linked to kernel and network. All of these commands are very practical and serve a significant purpose.

1) Command to know Network information

This single command can help you know a lot about your network. When you enter this command in your terminal information such as network status will be displayed in a split second.

Here is the format for this command:

root @ sample: ifconfig

 The output will display information such as IP address, subnet mask, and Physical MAC address. If you have used any third-party software such as VPN or Mac changer the customized values will be shown.

Sample output for the command:

inet   212.23.21.12 subnet 223.12.11.12 Broadcast 121.11.232.12

2) Command to know hardware information

This special command in Linux will help you know about a lot of static information about your system and kernel. You can know about a lot of details such as kernel type, Hardware processer information and operating system.

All you need to do is enter the following command:

root @ sample: uname {parameter}

You can enter -a as a parameter to display all of the information that the command can process.

However, if you are not comfortable with the terminal access of the information you can look at the same details using the Linux distro release file in the system folder.

3) Command to know details about the uptime

Uptime command serves a classical purpose to know information about system update time and other additional information that is necessary to be checked while dealing with the load of the system. This terminal command will help us to react to the resource shortage easily.

Here is the command:

root @ sample: uptime

The output will give valid information about the system running time as below:

12:23:12 up 23 min, 6 users, load average: 0.21, 0.03, 0.43

4) Command to free the resources

This command gives you the power to free the resources to stop sudden system halts. Sudden halts may affect a lot of services and processes that are going into the system. It is always necessary for a Linux administrator to track the resources.

Here is the command for format:

root @ sample: free -h

Here h parameter can be used to display the system information more reasonably and humanely.

5) Command to know about the users

Linux root user usually monitors a lot of users present in their command. To look at all the users Linux provides a command called 'who'. The command will also show the starting time when the user entered into the system.

Here is the command and output:

root @ sample: who

root 1 2019-07-12 23:12

6) Command to look at the past executed commands

Just like a browser provides history for all the websites you have visited Linux system also provides a command that displays 1000 of the latest command executed by the user in the system. You can also customize the number of commands to be displayed in the command configuration file.

Here is the command:

root @ sample: history

7) Command to display reports

Linux provides a special command to display and curate all the resources in the form of a report. This report analysis is complex and often requires advanced troubleshooting knowledge to understand the contents in the report. Sos report is a very important task to learn if you are a novice user.

A novice user can generate a sos report and send that file to an expert to make him solve minor problems remotely. However, for complex problems sos report may not effectively.

Here is the command:

root @ sample: sosreport

However, make sure you are ok with sending sensitive content to the remote Linux administrator.

With this, we have completed a detailed explanation about Linux system commands. In the next section, we will discuss directory commands which are necessary to be an expert Linux administrator.

Directory commands

The working directory is most important to be determined to execute commands in the system. During installation procedures or complex tasks such as compressing require to enter details about the working directory. We will also talk about commands that can help us change the working directory. Beginners should try to be perfect at directory commands for improving their expertise.

1) Command to know the present directory

This command can be used to display the present directory you are in. It is simply designated as pwd and displays the working directory you are located with exact precision.

Here is the command for it:

root @ sample: pwd

The output will be like:

/home/samplefolder

2) Command to switch the working directory

This is the most used command in Linux. By using this command, you can easily switch your directory. This is often the most used command because when using the Linux shell window. It is easy and flexible and can help you switch your directories.

Here are some of the additional functionalities that command provides:

a) cd- ---> You can use this parameter to shift to the previous directory

b) cd.. ----> With this parameter you can easily shift to an upper directory

c) cd~ ---- > By using this parameter you can at one instance fly to the present user's home directory. You can also fly to any user's home directory by adding the user name at the end of the command.

Here is the command:

root @ sample: cd   /home/sampleanalys

3) Command to view the details of the working directory

This command helps you to look at all the files that are present in the directory. You can use different parameters to look at files based on your preferences. By using a parameter such as -a you can even look at hidden files.

Here is the command:

root @ sample: ls -a

This command will display all the files that are present. If there are many files in the directory. It may take a little bit of time to show the results.

File directory management is an essential skill to learn. I hope you have learned valid information in this section. The next section will deal with a bundle of text commands for your easy handling of resources. Follow along!

Text Commands

Text is one of the most used ways to exchange information. Text files can be easily read in Linux using a lot of commands it provides. In this section, we will discuss in detail some of the most useful text commands. Follow along!

1) cat

This command can be used to read small plain text files. This is usually used by the Linux administrators because a lot of text files have very fewer lines. You can also use the parameter -n to display line numbers.

Here is the command for the said Linux function:

root @ sample: cat -n examplefile.txt

2) more

cat is designed for small text files and can become very buggy when used for long text files. So, for long configuration files, it is recommended to use more command which is specially designed for this functionality. This command window will also display the percentage bar which represents the percentage you have read till then.

Here is the command for the said Linux function:

root @ sample: more examplefile.txt

3) head

Head is a Linux text command that can be used to read customized lines in the top section of the text file. This can be very handy while checking text documents. Parameter -n defines the number of lines that can be read using this command.

Here is the command for the said Linux function:

root @ sample head -n 15 examplefile.txt

4) tail

The tail is a Linux text command that works in the exact opposite way of head command. When you use the tail command you can read the end part of the text document. As before, you can use -n parameter to define the number of lines that can be read using this command. Tail command can be especially handy

Here is the command for the said Linux function:

root @ sample: tail -n 15 examplefile.txt

5) tr

This is a special Linux text command that can be used to replace the characters in a text file. You might have found this functionality in Microsoft word. Here we can easily replace the manual text using various parameters. You can even replace two characters with the same character at once. All you need to do is learn about additional logical operators to implement it in this command functionality.

Here is the command:

root @ sample: cat example.txt tr a b

6) wc

This is a special Linux text file command that can be used to count the lines, text or bytes. All you need to do is select the parameter to count. You can just give the destination for the command and rest will be taken care of.

Here is the command:

root @ sample: wc   /home/newfolder/samplefile.txt

The output will show the count information.

7) stat

The stat is a special text command that can be used to view information such as storage information and time that the text document is created.

Here is the command for the above function:

root @ sample: stat examplefile.txt

This will display the above-said information.

8) cut

When there is a text file with a lot of information it is often difficult to read it. Sometimes u need to cut the text into half or different columns. By using this command, you can easily perform this action.

Here is the command:

root @ sample: cut -n 2 /home/example.txt

Here -n parameter defines the number of columns that can be divided.

9) diff

This is a special text command that can be used to find differences between the text files. This can be used to compare drafts that have been updated. This is very handy and can help you focus on what is different.

Here is the procedure:

1) First of all, view both the files you want to compare using the cat command.

2) After that using the diff command compare both the files and the results will be displayed after processing.

Here is the command:

root @ sample: cat example1.txt

root @ sample: cat example2.txt

root @ sample: diff --brief example1.txt example2.txt

With this, we have completed a brief and thorough explanation about the Text commands.

I hope you have learned valuable information about Linux commands dealing with different functionalities. In the next chapter, we will discuss SSH and other networking functionalities   in   Linux.

Chapter 5: Internet in Linux

In today's world networks are the most important for the functioning of the world. The largest network Internet is built by connecting systems using different protocols and communication mechanisms. While learning about an operating system it is necessary to know about all the networking features it offers.

Linux offers a lot of protocols to exchange data when connected to a network. They are much more safely encrypted with keys than the usual user and password combination. In this chapter, we will discuss in detail about SSH and other transfer protocols available in Linux systems in detail.

SSH is abbreviated as a secure shell and is developed to send commands to a remote machine that you are associated with. This is handy when working in teams and while trying to send commands that can easily manipulate the system.

SSH is known for its encrypted communication. Every message that is transferred cannot be hijacked by attackers. A lot of Linux applications that are used to exchange remote information use this protocol.

Before diving into deep about SSH in Linux we will discuss some of the basic networking concepts that are essential for a Linux learner. Follow along!

How can we identify systems in a network?

Using an IP address. Internet protocol address is designed to easily identify the system in a network and send signals to it. There are different IP versions such as IPv4 and IPv6.

Apart from the network address, every system (A mobile, a laptop or a personal computer) connected consists of a designated physical address known as MAC address. These are often not easy to tamper, unlike an IP address.

Websites are also part of a huge network called the Internet and are often represented by an IP address. But it is not practically possible to remember every IP address for the website you are trying to visit so they are represented using a phone book like system called DNS where IP address is represented by a domain which we usually use in our daily life.

Some basic Linux Networking commands

This section will give you some basic commands that are usually used to perform basic networking tasks. Don't get overwhelmed by the commands as we will discuss these commands in detail in the next chapters.

a) How to find your IP address?

Every Linux system is assigned a network address and can be easily known using the following command.

Open your shell and enter the command

ifconfig

When you click enter you will get an output showing different parameters.

Here is the sample output:

indet addr ----c 164.232.12.1

HWaddr---- 23:ab:23:45:f3:6r

You can use the following command to get the default gateway of your system:

ip route

b) How to get assigned with an IP address

The previous section explains to you about finding the IP address of your system and in this section, we will discuss getting assigned with an IP address in the first place.

Usually, IP addresses are assigned in Linux using a DHCP server. It takes a lot of time to manually arrange a network address for the system. For this exact reason to make things easy for the user and to avoid address conflicts, Linux uses the DHCP server to automatically assign an IP address that is not identical to any other present in the network.

As soon as you are connected to an Ethernet connecting a new IP address is assigned using the DHCP server. However, if you are still not able to get connected with a network address you can use the following command to force assign the network address.

sudo dhclient

You also have a chance to release an IP address and assign a different one. You can use different commands to achieve the following objective.

Here is the command for it:

sudo dhclient -r

The IP addresses assigned with the help of the DHCP server are usually dynamic. They change very fastly and whenever you try to check the IP address they might have changed. It functions automatically and assigns a network address that is available from the pool of addresses.

For example, if you are in a university that has a private network every system connected is given a dynamic IP address that changes continuously in some significant time to get advanced security to the systems.

Note:

Some servers/websites need the static address to implement the functionalities they are offering. Static means network address that doesn't change. You can assign a static address using the following procedure.

This takes place through the graphical interface the Linux offers. Enter the gateway, IP address and subnet mask in the interface and click Enter to make the changes happen.

Next, we will learn how to configure services on Linux systems. However, before this, smooth communication between hosts must be ensured. If the network does not work, users will not be able to access it smoothly even if the service is deployed correctly. Therefore, configuring the network and ensuring the connectivity of the network are the last important knowledge points before learning to deploy Linux services.

Network Manager

A lot of Linux distros by default uses Network Manager to provide network services. This is a daemon process that dynamically manages network configuration and can keep network devices connected. Network Manager services can be managed using nmcli commands. Nmcli is a command-line based network configuration tool with rich functions and numerous parameters.

It can easily view network information or network status:

[root@sample ~]# nmcli connection show

Also, the Linux system supports network session function, allowing users to switch quickly among multiple configuration files (very similar to zone technology in firewall service).

If we need to manually specify the IP address of the network when using a notebook computer in the company network, we will use DHCP to automatically assign the IP address when returning home. This requires troublesome and frequent modification of IP addresses, but it is much simpler after using the network session function-the automatic switching of network configuration information can be realized only by activating corresponding network sessions in different use environments.

You can use the nmcli command and create a network session in the format "connectionaddcon-nametypeifname." Use the con-name parameter to specify the network session name company used by the company, and then use the ifname parameter to specify the network card name of the machine in turn. Use the autoconnect no parameter to set the default that the network session is not automatically activated, and use the ip4 and gw4 parameters to manually specify the IP address of the network.

[root@sample ~]# nmcli connection add con-name {enternamehere} ifname {procedure}

The network session configured with nmcli command is permanent, so when we go home from work, we can start the house network session conveniently, and the network card can automatically obtain the IP address through DHCP.

If you are using a virtual machine, please switch the network card (network adapter) of the virtual machine system to the bridging mode and restart the virtual machine system.

SSH

SSH (Secure Shell) is a protocol that can securely provide remote login and is currently the preferred way to remotely manage Linux systems. Before this, FTP or Telnet was generally used for remote login. However, because they transmit the account password and data information in clear text in the network, they are very insecure and vulnerable to man-in-the-middle attacks initiated by hackers. This will either tamper with the transmitted data information or directly capture the server's account password.

If you want to use the SSH protocol to remotely manage Linux systems, you need to deploy and configure sshd service programs. Sshd is a remote management service program developed based on SSH protocol. It is not only convenient and fast to use but also can provide two methods of security verification:

a) Password-based authentication - use the account and password to authenticate login;

b) Key-based authentication - a key pair needs to be generated locally, and then the public key in the key pair is uploaded to the server and compared with the public key in the server. This method is safer than that.

The preceding paragraph has emphasized many times that "everything in the Linux system is a file", so modifying the operating parameters of service programs in the Linux system is a process of modifying program configuration files.

The configuration information of sshd service is saved in /etc/ssh/sshd_config file. Operation and maintenance personnel usually refer to the file that holds the most important configuration information as the main configuration file, and the configuration file has many comment lines beginning with the good number. For these configuration parameters to take effect, the previous well number needs to be removed after the parameters are modified.

Here is the command to start the SSH service on a specific IP address.

[root@sample ~]# **ssh 162.34.232.12**

If it is forbidden to log in to the server remotely as root administrator, the probability of password cracking by hackers will be greatly reduced. First, use Vim text editor to open the main configuration file of sshd service, then remove the pound sign (#) before the yes parameter in line 34, and change the parameter value yes to no, so root administrator is no longer allowed to log in remotely. Remember to finally save the file and exit.

Again, the general service program does not get the latest parameters immediately after the configuration file is modified. If you want the new configuration file to take effect, you need to restart the corresponding service program manually. It is better to add this service program to the startup item so that the service program will automatically run and continue to provide services to users when the system starts next time.

[root@sample~]# restart sshd

[root@sample ~]# enable sshd

In this way, when the root administrator tries to access the sshd service program again, the system will prompt an inaccessible error message. Although the parameters of sshd service program are relatively simple, this is the correct way to configure service program in Linux system. All we have to do is to draw inferences from other examples and learn how to use them flexibly, so that even if we encounter unfamiliar services later, we can still handle them.

SSH key based authentication

As explained in the previous section SSH service key-based authentication is one of the most popular services used in Linux. To use key based authentication, you are required to upload the public key that is encoded to SSH server.

Always create keys as a normal user as root restrictions can make others not accessible to the authentication.

Here we explain the step by step procedure to generate and import SSH keys:

1) In the first step we will create a keypair that has an option to enter passphrase. You need to confirm the passphrase and your encrypted key will be generated.

Here is the command:

root @ sample: ssh -keygen

2) You can also generate a key without a passphrase. However, it is advised to use a passphrase it gives an additional layer of security while using the SSH service.

3) Now in the next step you need to carefully import the key to the remote system. Here is the command to make it happen without any hiccups.

ssh-copy-id sk@132.23.22.11

You can disable it if you ever want to not deal with key based SSH.

Connecting via Telnet

Telenet is a famous Linux network administration tool which can help us to connect to a remote computer with an authentication procedure. Telnet has the power to control the Remote computer with no restrictions just like SSH. Although, not being as secure as SSH it still has its merits.

First of all, it is easy to install and comes inbuilt with many Linux distros. If you are not provided with Telnet you can install it via wget downloader.

The mechanism of Telnet is it uses basic password authentication mode. Use the following command to connect to the Telnet.

root @ sample: telnet {enter the host name}

Here host name refers to the ip address of the remote machine we are trying to connect to.

For example, you can connect to Localhost to connect to computers in the same network.

root @ sample: telnet localhost

After this in the command we will receive a prompt to enter the username and password.

After a successful connection you can further execute the commands to run in the remote machine. Telnet can be easily ended using the logout command as given below.

root @ sample: telnet logout

Encryption

Encryption is a technique for encoding and decoding information. It converts plaintext information that could have been read directly into ciphertext form through a certain algorithm (key). The key is the key of the ciphertext, which is divided into a private key and public key. When transmitting data, if you are worried about being monitored or intercepted by others, you can encrypt the data with the public key before transmission, and then transmit it. In this way, only the user who has the private key can decrypt the data, and even if other people intercept the data, it is generally difficult to decrypt it into clear text information.

In a word, using passwords to verify passwords in a production environment is always at risk of being hacked or intercepted by sniffers. If the key authentication method is correctly configured, the sshd service program will be more secure. We will make the following specific configuration, and the steps are as follows.

Step 1: Generate a "key pair" in the client host.

Step 2: Transfer the public key file generated in the client host to the remote host:

Step 3: Set the server to allow only key authentication and reject the traditional password authentication method. Remember to save and restart the sshd service program after modifying the configuration file.

Step 4: When the client attempts to log in to the server, it can log in successfully without entering a password.

SCP

Scp(secure copy) is a command for secure transmission between networks based on SSH protocol.

Its format is "scp [Parameters] Local File Remote Account @ Remote IP Address: Remote Directory".

Different from the cp command explained cp command can only copy files in the local hard disk, and scp can not only transmit data through the network but also encrypt all data. For example, if you want to transfer some files from one host to another via the network, and the two hosts happen to be Linux systems, then you can easily transfer the files by using scp command.

When using scp command to copy files from local to remote host, it is first necessary to write down the storage location of local files in the form of an absolute path. If you want to transfer all the data in the entire folder, you also need to add the parameter -r for the recursive operation.

Then write down the IP address of the remote host to be transmitted, and the remote server will require authentication. The current user name is called root, and the password is the password of the remote server. If you want to use the identity of the specified user for authentication, you can use the parameter format of user name @ host address.

Finally, you need to add a colon after the IP address of the remote host and write down which folder to send to the remote host. As long as the parameters are correct and the user's identity is successfully verified, the transfer can begin.

Also, the scp command can be used to download files from the remote host to the localhost. For example, you can download the system version information file of the remote host, so you don't need to log in to the remote host first and then transfer the file, which saves a lot of trouble. When learning sshd service when the session with the remote host is closed, the command running on the remote host is also interrupted.

If we are using commands to package files, or using scripts to install a service program, we must never close the terminal window opened locally or disconnect the network link in the middle. Even fluctuations in network speed may cause the task to be interrupted.

At this time, we can only restart the remote link and restart the task. There also times when we are performing a file packaging operation and want to install a service program with scripts. At this time, because the output information of the packaging operation fills up the user's screen interface, we can only open another terminal window for the remote session.

With this, we have given a layman introduction to some of the most advanced concepts in the Linux system. The Internet in Linux is a huge topic and needs continuous reading knowledge to enhance skills in this medium.

We recommend you to use various websites and books to expand your knowledge in the expertise. In the next chapter, we will start discussing Linux commands in detail along with a lot of examples. Follow along to improve your Linux administration skills exponentially. By the end of this chapter, most of the theoretical knowledge is completed and from now we recommend you to use your Linux system and experiment with the commands we are discussing. Follow along!

Chapter 6: Extra Features in Linux

This chapter is a comprehensive guide that explains about various individual features that Linux systems possess. We will discuss topics such as directory permissions, Compressing, and file systems in detail along with commands whenever we feel necessary. This chapter will further expand into chapters that deal with more complex topics in Linux. Follow along!

File and directory permissions

Linux is a professional operating system that is often used in enterprises and industries with a lot of users. Giving permissions to everyone will lead to a catastrophe. Hackers can also manipulate one employee to get access to the whole system. For this exact reason, Linux provides users with a set of comprehensive file and directory permissions.

This section will help you understand how Linux deals with multiple users and groups and also some commands that will help you understand the mechanism. At first, we will discuss in detail about the types of users that are present in Linux.

1) Root user

The root user is the admin or controller of the system. The root user is often powerful and can edit or change any file contents in the system. He is also responsible for maintaining every other user in the system. If someone gets access to the root user then he has attained the power to destroy the whole system.

2) Normal users

These are the other set of users that are present under the root base. Normal users are usually divided into groups by the root user and are given separate permissions according to their requirements. For example, in an IT company programmers are only given access to the project files that they are working on whereas Security analysts are given access to all the projects that the company is working on.

Types of permissions

Linux or any other operating system usually gives the following three permissions to their users according to their decision.

1) Read

Users allocated to this permission level can only read the contents that are present. They are not allowed to edit the files by any means. These users are called Lower access system users.

2) Read and Write

Users allocated to this permission level can not only read the system files but can also write the files.

3) Read, write and execute

Users allocated to this permission level can not only read and write but also execute the programs. Root users usually don't give these permissions for users due to its sensitive nature.

Here are some ways to grant permissions to both the individual owner and a group

1) chown

This is a command that permits an individual user.

chown [usernmae] [location]

In the username, column enter the username you are thinking of giving the permission to and in the location enter the location/name of the file that you are using.

2) chgrp

This is another command that is used to allot permission to a group. As discussed before in an enterprise some groups of users are allowed to access only a few of the functionalities. For example, programmers can only access the project files whereas testers can get access to everything that a project holds.

Root users use chgrp to give programmers group to access program files. Here is the command

chgrp [groupname]

In the previous section, we have discussed allowing permissions and in the next section, we will discuss commands that will help us to confirm whether the permissions have been alloted or not. Follow along!

You can use the following commands to check the permission of the file you want to.

1) ls

ls -l [filename]

When we enter the following command the system automatically defines the permission status.

2)stat

stat [filename]

Changing permissions using chmod

chmod is often used by programmers while using Linux systems to change the permissions. chmod gives complete access to the system and can only be executed by the root user.

chmod 777 [filename]

Are you confused about what 777 represents?

Read -4

Write - 2

Execute - 1

If all the three are added then it is 7 and the three 7 represents that the changes are being made to all the three owners, group and all other uses. So, by entering 777 permission changes all over the system.

In the next section, we will discuss compressing and archiving in detail along with a lot of examples.

Compressing and archiving

Before discussing various commands that can compress files in Linux it makes sense to know a bit of compressing.

What is compressing?

Compressing is a process in which the file size is reduced by various algorithms and techniques. If you are a

Windows user you might have probably used software like WinRAR which uses compression techniques to reduce the size. Popular compression formats are rar, zip,7z.

However, Linux uses a much more complex compression format known as tar. Linux compression is usually of two types.

1) Lossy

Lossy is a type of compression technique in which the desired file is decreased in size by losing some of its content. For example, we can turn an mp4 file into a 3gp video file using the following compression techniques. In the lossy compression even though the quality is reduced essence of the file can be still understood. The lossy type of compression is famously used for multimedia files.

2) Lossless

Lossless compression is another type of compression technique where data needs to be compressed without losing any essence. For example, a text document that has valuable information cannot be compressed by lossy technique because the document may get corrupted and lose some information. Even of not being an effective compression technique Linux is said to use this.

a) Tar command

The most important thing to do while compressing is to archive them at first. We will use tar command to archive the files. Tar is known as tape archive popularly. We will discuss about tar command in detail in the next chapters.

File system and storage device management

The file system is an important way to categorize a system. Both Windows and Mac use different procedures to maintain their file system. Linux uses a different perspective to use the file system in the operating system. We will learn about some of these concepts in brief in this section.

Windows and other operating systems use a physical drive option that is represented by a letter and a storage space. However, Linux uses a tree structure to represent its file system. /root is often described as the top of the tree system in the Linux.

If any other physical hard drives need to be installed then they are usually mounted for the usage. After the usage of the hard drive, they can be easily unmounted.

Where the devices are represented?

In windows when a hard drive is inserted they are usually shown in the devices section if necessary drivers are installed. Linux, however, represents all the devices in the /dev directory.

For practical experimentation, you can simply enter the following command in your Linux terminal to look at all the devices that are present

The command is here:

cd /dev

ls -l

How Linux represents devices?

Linux in the olden times is said to represent floppy drives and Hard drives using fd0, hda representation.

Now a day, we are getting a hard disk drive that uses SATA partition system. These are represented using the name sda,sdb,sdc etc...

Here a,b,c represents the serialization concept the Linux file system uses. a is represented as the first hard drive, b as the second hard drive and so on.

Even these hard drives can be further divided according to the partitions and can be easily represented using sda1,sda2,sda3, etc...

Linux sometimes cannot format the drives easily because they support the NTFS file system which is easily accessible by windows. This is the reason why windows operating systems can format the devices easily and Linux which supports file systems such as ext1, ext2,ext3.. as they need to convert the file system first.

To get thorough expertise on Linux file systems you need to learn in detail about mounting and unmounting along with the commands. Follow along!

What is mounting?

Mounting is a process that makes the Linux system recognize the hardware device. Usually windows automatically identify the hardware devices. Whereas, Linux uses a mounting option to identify the devices.

What is unmouting?

Unmounting is the option that needs to be used to remove a system from the system. It is similar to the eject option in the windows. It is not mandatory to use unmount before removing external hard drives but it is recommended normally.

Becoming secure and anonymous

Safety is an important concern for internet and computer users now a days. Even being reputed companies Windows and Apple are often criticized for collecting a lot of data from their users. Whatever their intention maybe it is obvious that now a days our data is not safe.

Linux on the other side an open source operating system without any enterprises is often well known for its anonymous features. A lot of hackers prefer Linux due to its advanced features and tools that will not make them vulnerable to their internet service providers. As a Linux beginner it is often important to get a good knowledge about anonymous services that Linux offers. Follow along to know more about it in detail.

Tracking

Almost everything you do can be tracked by your government or ISP. There are certain firewalls that restrict you to access websites I. Your country due to the country censor.

How are they tracked?

Every information you send via internet is sent via a packet. Packet consists of your ip address and the destination address. So, if your providers check the log files then it is easy to trace back to you.

How to get away from tracking?

We Will provide you three best ways to escape from the tracking and live an anonymous life in the internet. All these methods are practically proved to increase your privacy and safety.

a) Proxy servers

Proxy as known by everyone is a middle man between the communication. When you are trying to send a message or request to the destination the packet travels through the proxy server and reaches the destination. So, the destination recognizes the proxy server as the primary requester and sends the information to it. You can get private and public proxies for better management of your internet usage.

After receiving the response, the proxy server sends us the response which we will see through a browser or a web application. This exact procedure can help you to keep you anonymous.

b) TOR proxy

TOR is one of the famous anonymous clients that can help you extra safe from the internet tracking. TOR can also be used to look at the dark web. TOR is a project developed by independent Network engineers to bundle that proxy chains from a lot of computers. When you start a TOR service in your system all your data will be sent to a TOR proxy available and will further be sent to multiple secret TOR proxies available all around the world.

Even if the government try to check the logs it will be very difficult to trace your roots. TOR is however slow due to a lot of requests receiving by the proxy server.

C) VPN

VPN is also another way to encrypt your information. VPN can make you access blocked websites. By using a virtual private network, you can easily become anonymous.

There are several premium VPN services such as Hide my ass, Nord VPN.

Automating tasks

Automation is one of the pioneer reasons for the adaptation of Linux in server technologies and database maintenance. A lot of system administrators use automated scripts to check the necessary requirements for a system. Automating not only saves time but helps us to understand things from a different perspective. In the next section we will discuss some concepts that can help us create automated tasks.

crontab & cron daemon

In Linux there is a process called as cron daemon that can take parameters to execute after a particular time or if it can satisfy a condition.

Daemon as discussed before is a background process that can manipulate system. Linux users can enter a command to schedule their task for a particular time in the crontab.

112

And when the time comes cron daemon that is running in the background initiates the procedure. For example, we can use crontab to shut down the system after 30mins inactivity. All you need to do is add this on the crontab.

Crontab can perform tasks even after few years and months. You can find various parameters of the crontab to do complex operations such as deleting the log files after a reboot etc.,

While automated tasks can be used to done to various tasks it is recommended to use this feature to back up your data.

Backing up

Backup is very essential for users using Linux as they may contain sensitive information. However, people are often probe to forget this simple task. It is recommended to back up your files once in a week. With the help of crontab you can schedule backup for your desired time.

Here is the command:

crontab backup time

With this we have completed a comprehensive chapter that describes everything about Linux extra features. In the next chapter we will discuss in detail about process management. Follow Along!

Chapter 7: Process Management in Linux

First of all, before diving into deep about different commands that are used in process management, we need to get a good idea about what a process means.

What is the process?

Generally, an operating system is compiled with the help of certain programs to solve different tasks. All of these programs are systematically arranged with the help of a graphical user interface that acts as a medium to perform tasks.

Programs are a step by step instructions to solve a problem. Programmers use logical and analytical algorithms to create complex programs that can handle different instructions. When a program is started it is stored in the main memory and starts executing.

Whenever programs start or initiate itself it is called a process. Processes are usually represented by ids by the operating systems for better monitoring of resources.

115

Linux operating system uses various advanced system techniques to handle and prioritize processes. In this chapter, we will discuss in detail about different use cases of processes with the help of Linux commands. Follow along!

Process id:

Process id also abbreviated as PID is usually represented by numbers for a process in the Linux systems. Every process is designated to have a PID. The first system process that Linux starts during the booting procedure has a PID 1 and all other processes have much longer PIDs.

Usually, parent processes and children processes can be easily identified as PID's of parent processes are shorter and PID's of child processes are longer.

Parent process

The parent process is a type of process that initiates system calls using fork () function. When fork () function is used child processes can be easily initiated.

For example, when LibreOffice is opened in Linux a parent process starts. After some time the user clicks Check for updates in the interface and the parent process calls a system function fork () to initiate a child process that checks for updates.

One parent process can start multiple child processes. However, an infinite number of child processes is not a problem as system resources may get stuck with the sudden volume.

Child Process

The child process is a process that is often initiated by a parent process. It is usually similar to the parent process in many ways and even has a similar PID. If by any chance a child process is ended or interrupted a signal will be sent to the parent process to know about it. Child processes are often called by fork() and often ends by themself. This self-destruction can help save memory resources for the system.

Pstree

pstree is a command in Linux that shows the tree process structure or the sequential process structure that the Linux system possesses.

pstree is categorically organized so that we can see the first processes to the endpoint. All the processes are arranged in a way that the child process and parent process can be easily noticeable.

Command is here:

pstree

Open your command and enter the above command to look at the tree structure of all the processes running in your Linux system.

PS command

PS also called a process status command is a special Linux utility that is used to display all the processes that are present based on multiple parameters.ps command has become a Linux administrator handy tool because it can help to filter the processes according to their requirements.

In this section, we will describe some commands that can help you understand the scope of ps command. It is advised to enter the commands on your Linux system for a customized learning experience.

a) ps

This is the basic command that can be used to display all the processes that are present in the current shell. Remember that this plain ps command will only display the processes that are running on the present shell but not on the entire system. This becomes hand when you are focused on a batch of processes that you have initiated before.

Command here:

ps

b) Display all processes

These set of commands can be used to display processes that are at present running in the Linux system. They can be made to display in various formats too.

i) ps -e

This command displays all the process that are present in the linux system. Enter the following command to dispay PID, Time of the process.

2) ps -ef

This command also displays al the processes but in a way such that PPID is present.

3) ps -x

With this command, you can display every process that is being represented by the user. If you are a root user this will display every process that is running on the system

4) *Display processes of a certain user*

In this command line execution, all the processes of a specific user will be displayed. All you need to do is get root access and enter the following command format to get all the processes that are processed by the user

ps -fu [username]

ps -fu Raymond

Output will display all the processes that are run by the Raymond.

5) All the processes run with root access

This is a special command which helps us to display all the processes that are run with root privilege. Please enter the following command as a root user to look at all the processes you are running

ps -U root -u root

6) All the processes run by a group

As explained before the Linux system also supports groups that are a curative collection of users. By using the following command you will display all the processes that are being run by a particular group in the system.

ps -fG programmers

These are some of the examples that ps command offers in the Linux system. Mastering ps command can help Linux administrators.

Foreground and background processes

Usually, when we are working in a shell in the Linux system you can't initiate a process until the one that is opened is closed. These type of processes are called a foreground process and usually freezes the shell until the process is closed.

For example, enter the command that lists all the 50,000 files that are present in a directory.

All you need to enter is the following command in the directory location

ls

Because there are so many files to display the process takes some time to display the information of the files. Meanwhile if you observe you can't do anything in the shell window because it is freeze due to the ongoing foreground process.

However, the Linux system provides an option for you to run any process as a background process. All you need to do is enter the command give a space and enter the ampersand symbol and execute the command. With this, you can easily run any process as a background process.

Here is the command

ls &

Daemons

Daemons processes are the type of processes that are usually run in background without the user notifying it. This specific process is very highly responsible for all the functionalities that the software's offer.

init process

Init process is a special process that is usually started during the booting procedure of the Linux system. It has a PID of 1 and init process is started by the kernal. init process is like the mother of all processes that are present in the Linux system.

Process state life cycle

Like every entity in the Linux process also follows a life cycle. There are different stages in the life of a process according to the Linux guides. Even if they are not practically visible to us learning about the Process lifecycle can help you look at things from a different perspective.

According to the resources, there are five stages in the life cycle of a process:

1) Running

This is the state where the designated process is ready to run or already started running upon the initiation.

2) Interruptible

Interruptible is a process lifecycle where it is waiting for others signals to proceed further. Child processes wait for the fork() system call from parent processes to proceed further. This is a perfect example for this process state.

3) Uninterruptible

This is a process state where the process is going to end due to the non-receiving signal from the process that need to do. This may occur due to overload on the resources or due to hardware problem. Process halts in this process.

4) Stopped

This is a process lifecycle where the process is automatically stopped or stopped by the root user. When the process ends system resources are freed and are allocated to other processes. However, you should be remembered that the stopped process can be easily restarted if wanted.

5) Zombie

This is a process life cycle in which the designated process gets terminated from the system and halts without any further response. However, when you look at the process tree structure the process can be found. These types of processes are known as zombie processes.

You can also look at top, kill and kill all commands which we have already discussed before. In the next chapter we will look at some of the advanced Linux commands in detail.

In the next section we will discuss in detail about Remote file system of the Linux. Process management system can help us to explore in depth about this topic.

Remote storage in Linux

Here we will give a step by instruction to the remote storage process using SSHFS client in Linux. Follow along!

Step 1:

First of all install sshfs client using any package manager. Here we will use yum to install the client.

yum install sshfs

Step 2:

Then create a directory using the mount system we have discussed before. You need to use mkdir to create a directory.

mkdır /mnt/foldername

Step 3:

In this step you need to link the resources to the remote store directory location. Here is the command for it.

sshfs {here enter the remote location directory} /mnt/homedirectory

After that you can check the mount directories using -hT parameter and can also unmount if you want to stop the functionalities.

With this we have completed a brief description about Linux process management. In the next chapter we will discuss about some of the advanced Linux commands in detail.

Chapter 8: Commands and Functions to master

So far, our study of Linux commands is like consolidating the foundation. Although there are no results on the surface for the time being everyone's internal skills are already quite strong. In the daily operation and maintenance of the Linux system, it is also necessary to master the operations of creating, modifying, and copying, cutting, renaming and deleting files.

Must Known Commands

1. touch command

The touch function can help us to create a blank file or set the time of the file in the format "touch [Options] [File]".

When it comes to creating blank text files, the touch command is quite simple, so simple that there is no need to spread it out. For example, the touch example command can create a blank text file called example in a split second.

For the touch command, the difficult operations are mainly reflected in setting the modification time (mtime) of file contents, the change time (ctime) of file permissions or attributes, and the reading time (atime) of files.

Next, we first use the ls command to check the modification time of a file, then modify the file, and finally use the touch command to set the modified file time to the time before modification (which is what many hackers do):

[root@sample ~]# ls -l file.cfg

[root@sample ~]# ls -l ks.cfg

2. mkdir command

The mkdir function can help us to create a blank directory in the format "mkdir [options] directory."

A folder is one of the most common file types in the Linux system. In addition to creating a single blank directory, this can also recursively create file directories with nested overlay relationships by combining the -p parameter.

[root@sample ~]# mkdir samplefolder

[root@sample ~]# cd samplefolder

[root@sample samplefolder]# mkdir -p

3 cp command

The cp command is used for exactly changing files or directories. This is one of the most important command as it deals with different additional advantage.

Everyone should be familiar with the file copy operation. In a Linux system, the copy operation can be divided into three specific situations:

a) The file you are dealing with is a directory, the source file will be copied to the directory;

b) The file you are dealing with is also a normal file, you will be asked if you want to overwrite it.

c) If the file you are working upon does not exist, the normal copy operation is performed.

Next, use touch to create an ordinary blank file named extra.log, then copy it into a backup file named y.log finally, use ls command to view the files in the directory:

[root@sample ~]# touch extra.log

[root@sample ~]# cp extra.log y.log

[root@sample ~]# ls

extra.log y.log

4 mv command

The mv function can help us to cut or change the name of the file in the format "mv [parameters] {This is where it exists} [Destination Path | Destination File Name]".

Cut operation is different from copy operation because it will delete the source file by default and only keep the cut file.

If you cut a file in the same directory, you are renaming it:

[root@sample~]# mv y.log extra.log

[root@sample ~]# ls

extra.log linux.log

5 rm

The rm command is especially developed for erasing a file or directory in the deal rm [parameter] file.

When deleting files in the Linux system, the system will ask you by default if you want to delete it. If you don't want to see this kind of repeated confirmation information all the time, you can follow the -f parameter after rm command to force deletion.

Also, if you want to delete a directory, you need to add a -r parameter after the rm command, otherwise, you cannot delete it.

Let's try to delete the previously created extra.log and linux.log files:

[root@sample ~]# rm linux.log

rm: remove regular empty file

[root@sample ~]# rm -f extra.log

[root@sample ~]# ls

[root@sample~]#

All the files are deleted with the help of the following Linux command.

6 dd order

Dd function can help us to copy files or convert files according to specified size and number of data blocks in the format of "dd [parameter]".

Dd command is an important and characteristic command, which enables users to copy the contents of files according to the specified size and number of data blocks. Of course, if you like, you can also convert the data in the copy process. There is a device file named /dev/zero in the Linux system, and every time it is explained in class, it is full of philosophical color.

Because this file does not occupy system storage space but can provide endless data, it can be used as an input file for dd commands to generate a file of a specified size.

For example, we can use the dd command to fetch a 2500MB data block from the /dev/first device file and then save the file named 2500_file.

After understanding this command, you can create files of any size at will:

[root@sample ~]# dd if=/dev/first of=2500_file count=1 bs=2500M

The function of dd command is not limited to copying files. If you want to make the optical disc in the optical drive device into an iso format image file, you need to use third-party software to do so in Windows system, but in Linux system, you can directly use dd command to suppress the optical disc image file and turn it into an iso image that can be used immediately:

[root@sample ~]# dd if=/dev/disc of=Mint-server sample.Com.iso

Considering that some readers will struggle with the relationship between the size of bs blocks and the number of count blocks, let's give an example to explain.

Assuming that appetite (i.e. demand) is a fixed value, the size of the spoon used to hold rice is bs pieces, while the number of times the spoon is used to hold rice is count pieces. The user needs to balance the size of the spoon (bs block size) with the number of times he uses the spoon (count block number) if he wants to eat (meet his needs). The bigger the spoon, the fewer times it is used to hold rice. As can be seen from the above, bs and count are both used to specify the size of the capacity. As long as the demand can be met, they can be combined and matched at will.

7 file command

The file function can help us to view the type of file in the format "filename".

In the Linux system, because the text, directories, devices and so on are all collectively called files, and we cannot know the specific file types by suffixes alone, then we need to use the file command to view the file types.

[root@sample ~]# file snake-ks.cfg

snake-ks.cfg: ASCII text

Due to different hardware or wrong operation, readers may make mistakes in the experimental configuration. Please be patient and take a closer look at the operation steps. Don't be discouraged. In the next section, we will discuss some of the advanced command functions in Linux.

Pack Compression and Search Commands

On the network, people are more and more inclined to transmit files in compressed format because the compressed files are small in size and the transmission time is short under the same network speed. Next, we will learn how to pack, compress and decompress files in Linux system, and let users search for matching information in text files based on keywords, and search for specific files based on specified names or attributes in the entire file system. Although there are only 3 commands in this section, its functions are complicated and have many parameters, so it is explained at the end of this chapter.

1. tar command

Tar is one of the advanced mechanisms that can be used to achieve deep compression in files. Checkout the below section to know more about it.

In a Linux system, there are many common file formats, among which. tar or. tar.gz or. tar.bz2 format is mainly used. We need not worry about too many formats to remember them. Most of these formats are generated by tar command.

First, the -c parameter is used to complete the necessary action, and the -x parameter is used to decompress the file, so these two parameters cannot be used simultaneously. Secondly, the -z parameter specifies to use the Gzip format to change files, and the -j parameter specifies to use the bzip2 format to do the same activity with files.

The user uses the suffix of the file to determine which format parameter should be used for decompression. When performing some advanced operations, it may take several hours. If the screen has not been output, on the one hand, you cannot judge the progress of packaging, on the other hand, you may suspect that the computer crashed.

Therefore, it is highly recommended to use the -v parameter to continuously display the advanced manipulation process to the user. The -C parameter is used to specify which specified directory to extract. The -f parameter is particularly important; it must be placed at the last bit of the parameter to represent the name of the package to be changed.

Let's demonstrate the operations of packing, compressing and decompressing one by one. First, the /etc directory is packed and compressed in gzip format by using tar command, and the file is named etc.tar.gz:

[root@sample ~]# tar example.gz /etc

Next, specify and extract the packed compressed package file into the /root/etc directory (use mkdir command to create the /root/etc directory first):

[root@sample ~]# mkdir /dev/example

[root@sample ~]# tar example.gz -C /dev/etc

2. grep order

The grep function can help us to perform keyword searches in text and display the matching results in the format "grep [options] [file]".

Grep command is the most widely used text search matching tool. Although there are many parameters, most of them are basically not used.

If the level of an IT training lecturer can only stay at the level of "technical porter" and cannot refine and summarize high-quality technical knowledge, it is not a good thing for his students. We will only talk about the two most commonly used parameters here: -n parameter is used to display the line number of the searched information; The -v parameter is used to deselect information (i.e. not all information rows containing keywords).

These two parameters can almost fulfill 80% of your work needs in the future. As for the other hundreds of parameters, even if they are encountered in the future, it is still too late to query them by using the man grep command.

In Linux system, the /etc/passwd file stores all user information, and once the user's login terminal is set to /sbin/nologin, login to the system is no longer allowed, so grep command can be used to find out all user information in the current system that is not allowed to login to the system:

[root@sample ~]# grep /etc/section /dev/example

3. find command

The find function can help us to find files according to the specified criteria, and the format is "find [find path] find criteria operation".

This book has mentioned many times that "everything in the Linux system is a file". In the Linux system, the search work is generally completed through the find command, which can use different file characteristics as search criteria (such as file name, size, modification time, permissions and other information). Once the matching is successful, the information will be displayed on the screen by default.

Here we need to focus on the important role of the -exec parameter. This parameter is used to hand over the results found by the find command to the following command for further processing. Because of the special requirements of the find command for parameters, although exec is in long format, it still only needs a minus sign (-).

According to the File system Hierarchy Standard protocol, configuration files in Linux systems are saved to the /etc directory. If you want to get a list of all files in the directory that start with host, you can execute the following command:

[root@sample ~]# find /dev -name "example*" -display

If you want to search the entire system for all files with SUID permissions, just use -2000:

[root@sample ~]# find / -select -2000 -display

Advanced Experiment: Find all files belonging to Linux users in the entire file system and copy them to the /root/results directory.

The focus of this experiment is "-exec {} \;" Parameter, where {} represents every file searched by the find command, and the command must end with "\".

With this we have given a good introduction to Linux advanced commands. In the next chapter we will discuss about Linux text editor in detail.

Chapter 9: Using Text editor in Linux

This chapter first explains how to use the Vim editor to write and modify documents, and then helps readers deepen many functions of the Vim editor by configuring the hostname; system network card and software warehouse parameter files one by one.

Also, in our daily work, we will have to write documents, which are all done through text editors.

Therefore, we choose to use the Vim text editor, which will be installed on all current Linux operating systems by default and is an excellent text editor.

Vim text editor

The reason why Vim can be recognized by many manufacturers and users is that there are three modes in Vim editor-command mode, end-line mode, and edit mode. Each mode supports a variety of different command shortcut keys, which greatly improves the work efficiency, and users will feel quite comfortable after getting used to it. To operate the text efficiently, we must first understand the operating differences among the three modes and the switching methods between the modes that have different functionalities.

When the Vim editor is run each time, the command mode is entered by default. At this time, it is necessary to switch to the desired interface for writing the document. However, after writing the document, it is necessary to return to the command mode before entering the last line mode to save or exit the document. In Vim, it is not possible to switch directly from the input mode to the last row mode.

This exact command is mainly used to save or exit files set the working environment of Vim editor, and allow users to execute external commands or jump to a specific number of lines in the written document. To switch to the last line mode, enter a colon in the command mode.

So far, everyone has a theoretical basis for writing documents in the Linux system. Next, we will begin to write a simple script document.

Writing a document using Vim

145

The first step in writing a script document is to give the document a name, which is called sample.txt If the document exists, it is opened. If it does not exist, a temporary input file is created.

Txt document, the command mode of Vim editor is entered by default. At this time, only the commands in this mode can be executed, and the text content cannot be input at will. We need to switch to the input mode to write the document.

As mentioned, three keys a, I and o can be used to switch from the command mode to the input mode respectively. Among them, the A key and the I key switch to the input mode at the back of the cursor and the current position of the cursor respectively, while the O key creates an empty line below the cursor. At this time, you can tap the A key to enter the input mode of the editor.

After entering the input mode, you can input the text content at will. Vim editor will not execute the text content you input as a command.

After writing, to save and exit, you must first hit the Esc key of the keyboard to return to the command mode from the input mode.

 Then enter: wq!

Switch to the last row mode to complete the save exit operation.

When entering: wq! Command, it means to force the document to be saved and exited. Then you can use cat command to view the saved document contents.

Is it very simple?! Continue editing this document. Since additional content is to be added below the original text content, it is more efficient to tap the o key in the command mode to enter the input mode.

Applications of Vim text editor

Next, three small tasks will be arranged for readers from shallow to deep. To thoroughly master the use of Vim editor, everyone must complete it one by one. Don't be lazy. If you forget the relevant commands during the completion of these three tasks, you can return to the previous section for further review and mastery.

To find a specific host in the local area network, or to distinguish between hosts, in addition to having an IP address, a host must be configured with a hostname, and hosts can access each other through this name similar to the domain name. In a Linux system, the hostname is mostly saved in the /etc/hostname file, and then the content of the /etc/hostname file is modified to "sample" as follows.

Step 1: use Vim editor to modify the "/etc/hostname" host name file.

Step 2: Delete the original host name and append "titlesample". Note that after modifying the host name file using Vim editor, it will be executed in the last line mode: wq! Command to save and exit the document.

Step 3: Save and exit the document, and then use the hostname command to check if the modification was successful.

[root@sample ~]# vim /etc/titlesample

sample

The hostname function can help us to view the current hostname, but sometimes the change of hostname will not be synchronized to the system immediately. Therefore, if the original hostname is displayed after modification, you can restart the virtual machine and view it again:

[root@sample ~]# titlesample

sample

Whether the IP address of the network card is configured correctly is the premise of whether the two servers can communicate with each other. In the Linux system, everything is filed, so the job of configuring network services is actually editing the network card configuration files.

Therefore, this small task can not only help you practice using Vim editor but also lay a solid foundation for you to learn various service configurations in Linux later. When you study this book carefully, you will feel a special sense of accomplishment, because the basic part in front of this book is very solid, while the content behind this book has almost the same network card IP address and operating environment, thus ensuring that you are fully committed to the study of various service programs without worrying about the problems of the system environment.

If you have a certain operation and maintenance experience or are familiar with the early Linux system, you will encounter some unacceptable differences in learning this book.

In other Linux system, the prefix of the network card configuration file is eth, the first network card is eth0, and the second network card is ET H1. And so on. In RHEL 7, the prefix of the network card configuration file starts with ifcfg, and the name of the network card together form the name of the network card configuration file, such as ifcfg-eno6746732; Fortunately, there is no big difference except the change of file name.

Now there is a network card device named ifcfg-eno6746732. we configure it to start up automatically, and the IP address, subnet, gateway and other information are manually specified. the steps should be as follows.

Step 1: First switch to the /etc/sample/network-scripts directory (where the network card configuration files are stored).

Step 2: use Vim editor to modify the network card file ifcfg-eno6746732, write the following configuration parameters one by one and save to exit. Since the hardware and architecture of each device are different, please use ifconfig command to confirm the default name of each network card.

Step 3: Restart the network service and test whether the network is connected.

Enter the directory where the network card configuration file is located, then edit the network card configuration file and fill in the following information:

```
[root@sample ~]# cd /var/example/rarfile
```

Execute the command to restart the network card device (there will be no prompt message under normal circumstances), and then test whether the network can be connected through ping command. Since the ping command does not automatically terminate in Linux systems, it is necessary to manually press Ctrl-c to forcibly end the process.

In this chapter we have given a good introduction to the text editor in Linux. In the next chapter we will discuss about python programming in detail. Follow along!

Chapter 10: Python programming for Linux

Linux uses scripting languages to automate tasks and perform functions that are often complex and tedious. Without these scripts, it would take developers and Linux administrators an infinite amount of time to secure the systems and perform checks. For this valid reason knowledge of scripting languages is a must for anyone who is trying to be proficient in Linux. There are many scripting languages such as Perl, Bash, Ruby, and Python.

Why Python?

With a lot of languages available to choose from it is often overwhelming for a beginner to choose a perfect language that fits for him. We are not forcing you to choose Python as a primary language because the choice of programing language is always personal. Always try different languages and choose the one which you are more comfortable with. However, as learned from different Linux programmers and administrators Python is one of the most preferred and loved scripting languages due to its versatility, simplicity, and robustness.

Python is also very easy to learn and there are a lot of resources available to master your programming skills and follow different open source projects to enhance your skills. Python is known for its adaptability according to situations as it can be used for both simple text analysis tasks and complex IP filtering tasks. Another reason for the success of python is it is extremely easy to read without a lot of indentation.

Python also has an excellent community that consists of an abundant number of third-party packages and automated scripts. With all these due reasons we strongly recommend you to try python to develop your Linux scripting skills.

In the next section, we will discuss the basics of python in detail. Python is a vast topic and there are many resources to further improve your skills. We in this section will discuss some topics that are essential for Linux scripting. Follow along!

Python Programming for Linux

Before knowing about python basics, it is recommended to learn about installing third party modules in the system. Modules make the programmer's life easy in a lot of ways. Python provided a module manager called pip for the easy installation of modules.

Use the following command to install pip

srujan> apt-get install python3 pip

pip3 install <modulename>

Use the following command to install any desired module. You can look at the GitHub or pip website to look at different modules available for download. A programmer's choice of modules also differs according to choose and comfortability dealing with the packages.

Every module consists of a text file that explains everything about that module and commands that can be used to execute the tasks. Experiment with modules and if you did face any error give a quick google search or ask support for the module community in GitHub.

There is also a package manager called wget that is used to download third-party modules form various domains.

With this, we have got a good understanding of the modules and in the next section; we will dive into scripting in detail.

Where to create python programs?

There are a lot of Python IDE's that are available to execute python programs. However, we recommend using JetBrains as one of the most simple and free IDE available for python programmers.

A suggestion:

Programming is not an easy task. It takes a lot of time to master the logical ability that programmers use to develop complex programs. Even experienced programmers often deal with errors. It is common to do mistakes and get stuck with debugging. Always look at it as a learning process and learn from your mistakes to create scripts that can accomplish your task.

Variables

Variables are a special entity which can be used to redo the same task or information. To be specific, variables are reusable data that can be used in different mathematical and string operations.

a =3

b = 'Example'

Comments

Comments are used to give an additional information to the program. They are usually created to help programmers. They are defined by # usually in the programs.

Here is an example:

This is a comment in python

Functions

Functions are an easy way to repeat the same task for many times. You can use function calls to call them whenever you want. For example, addition function can easily help you to add three numbers whenever possible.

Here is an example:

a=3

b = 2

fun(sum)

sum = a+b

Loops

Loops are an easy way to repeat the task again and again with a logical entity. There are many loops such as For,while and do-while loop.

Here is an example:

for (i=0)

a=2

b=4

if (a>2)

```
{

print(" This is done"

}
```

Control statements

Control statements are used to make a decision in programming. By using control statements, you can choose either between either true or false.

Here is an example:

```
if ( a>2)

print ( " This is red")

else

print(" This is white")
```

With this we have completed a brief description to python programming. You can even learn in depth about Classes and Objects in detail. Approach programming language as a weapon and use it to implement different tasks. In the next section we will discuss in depth about shell programming. Follow along!

Chapter 11: Advanced shell programming

Since we have learned almost all the basic and commonly used Linux commands in the previous chapters, the next task is to properly combine multiple Linux commands to make them work together so that we can process data more efficiently.

Before learning in detail about several advanced shell concepts we will discuss in detail about customizing the bash prompt. Follow along!

Customize Bash Prompt

Bash is usually boring to look at. So, to make your working bash environment enjoyable you can use different commands or changes to make the look change.

The most important thing to remember is to back up the ~/.bashrc file because this is where we are going to edit the content to change the look of bash shell.

You can use vi text editor to edit the content or you can use any other text editor of your choice.

PS1="sample> "

Add this command at the end of the file content and update the file. Now come to the Linux shell and execute it. You can see the change of the name in the bash interpreter shell. You can replace the Text of your choice.

You can even change colors and add emojis too in the bash interpreter shell. All you need to do is change the string file names and insert your desired color code or emoji code.

Interactive and Non-interactive shell

You should learn about the fact that there are usually three types of shells in the shell environment. They are Login shell, Interactive shell and Non-interactive shell respectively. We will discuss about these three shells in detail in this section.

a) Login shell

Login shell happens only when you do login into the system using SSH or by other means. By logging in it will load all the required entities that are necessary for the functioning. All of your custom environmental variables and bash functionalities will also be loaded.

b) Interactive shell

Interactive shell is a special shell where if you enter the shell type name it will start functioning.

For ex; in an interactive shell when you enter bash the bash environment will start its action.

c) Non-interactive shell

This is a different type of shell where shell interface doesn't even appear. Usually bash scripts automatically interact with this type of interfaces.

We had a good introduction to bash environment in the next section we will start discussing advanced topics such as Redirection commands, Aliases and environmental variables in detail.

Redirection commands

In short, input redirection refers to importing a file into a command, while output redirection refers to writing data information originally to be output to a screen into a specified file. In our daily study and work, we use output redirection more frequently than input redirection, so we divide output redirection into two different technologies: standard output redirection and error output redirection, and two modes: clear write and append write.

For example, we look at the attribute information of the two files respectively, and the second file does not exist. Although the operations for the two files will output some data information on the screen respectively, the difference between the two operations is very large:

[root@sample ~]# touch advance

[root@sample ~]# ls -l advance

ls: cannot access xxxxxx:

In the above command, a file named example exists, and the output information is some related rights and other

164

information of the file, which is also the standard output information of the command.

The second file named xxxxxx does not exist, so the error prompt message displayed after executing the ls command is also the error output message of the command. Then, if you want to transfer the data originally output to the screen to the file, you must treat the two kinds of output information differently.

Pipe

This pipe symbol is like a magic weapon. We can apply it to other different commands, such as viewing the file list and attribute information in the /etc directory in the form of page-turning (these contents will be displayed on the screen by default and cannot be clearly seen at all):

When modifying a user's password, it is usually necessary to enter the password twice for confirmation, which will become a very fatal flaw when writing automated scripts. By combining the pipe character with the --stdin parameter of the passwd command, we can use one command to complete the password reset operation:

```
[root@sample ~]# echo "advance" | user --input root
```

Do you think the pipeline operator command is a bit too late to learn? There are many ways to play pipeline symbols. For example, when sending an e-mail, the default method is interactive. We can use a command statement that combines pipeline symbols to "package" the edited content with the title, and finally, use this command to send the mail.

If readers are new to Linux, they may think that the above command combination is already very complicated, but readers who have experience in operation and maintenance will feel that they are not satisfied like scratching their boots. They hope to write more advanced and more powerful commands that are convenient.

For example, through redirection technology, multiple lines of information can be packaged and input or output at one time, making daily work more efficient.

Of course, we must not mistake the pipe command for being used only once in a command combination. We can use it like this: "First Command | Second Command | Third Command ".

Everyone may have encountered the embarrassment of forgetting to write. As Linux operation and maintenance personnel, we sometimes encounter situations where the name of a file is on the tip of our tongue but we just can't remember it. If you just remember the first few letters of a file and want to search all the files that start with this keyword, how do you do it?

For another example, suppose you want to view the relevant permission attributes of all hard disk files in batch, one way is as follows:

[root@sample ~]# ls -l /adv/attribute

Fortunately, we will only have 3 hard disk files and partitions. If there are several hundred, it is estimated that it will take me a day to do this. This shows that the efficiency of this method is really very low. Although we will only explain the storage structure and FHS of the

Linux system, we should be able to see some simple rules by now.

For example, these hard disk device files all start with sda and are stored in the /dev directory. thus, even if we do not know the partition number of the hard disk and the number of specific partitions, we can still use wildcard characters. As the name implies, wildcards are common symbols of matching information.

For example, asterisks (*) represent matching zero or more characters, and question marks (?) stands for matching a single character, the number [0-9] added in brackets stands for matching a single number between 0 and 9, and the letter [abc] added in brackets stands for matching any one of a, b and c.

In order to better understand the user's expression, the Shell interpreter also provides a particularly rich escape character to process the input special data.

The four most commonly used escape characters are as follows:

A backslash (\): Makes a variable following the backslash of a simple string.

Single quotation mark ("): Escape all variables as simple strings.

Double quotation marks ("): the variable attribute in them is retained without escape processing.

Back quotation mark (`'): returns the result after executing the command.

Create Alias

Alias are like speed dials in a Linux command interface. We often use commands and often use some commands very frequently. It is often frustrating to use them all over again in the command interface. Alias is an option that Linux provides to create custom shortcuts for your most used commands. Learning and mastering aliases can exponentially increase your productivity.

a) See current aliases

First of all, it is important to look at the existing aliases that are already present. So, enter the following commands to know about all of the existing aliases in the Linux system.

$ alias

$ ll

Now, all of the available aliases will be listed.

b) Create aliases

Creating aliases are pretty straightforward and easy. However, it is good if you can organize all the commands that you are using in a text file for a reference.

Here is the template for creating aliases:

alias {This is the short cut} = " Original Linux command"

Here is an actual Linux example for your reference.

alias sx = " cd /var/home/desktop"

However, you should remember that aliases are not permanent and can be uninstalled if you delete any system or bash files. There are some advanced techniques where you can create permanent aliases for the Linux kernel.

c) Delete aliases

There is also a command that can be used to easily delete aliases from the system.

Here is the command for it:

unalias {enter the alias name}

Example

unalias sx

With this we have given a good explanation about aliases in the next section we will discuss in detail about environmental variables.

Environmental variables

Variables are data types used by computer systems to hold variable values. In Linux systems, variable names are generally capitalized, which is a well-established norm. We can directly extract the corresponding variable value through the variable name.

The environment variables in Linux system are used to define some parameters of the system operating environment, such as different home directories and mail storage locations for each user.

The reason is self-evident-in order for the Linux system to run normally and provide services for users, hundreds of environment variables are needed to work together. We do not need to look at and learn each variable one by one, but we should concentrate on the most important content in a limited space.

In order to help the Linux system, build a working environment that can provide services to users through environment variables, hundreds of variables need to work together to complete. Of course, you don't need to read every variable, but you should tell readers the most important content in the most valuable books.

As mentioned earlier, everything is a file in the Linux system, and Linux commands are no exception. So, what exactly happened in Linux after the user executed a command? Simply put, the command execution in Linux is divided into 4 steps.

Step 1: Judge whether the user inputs a command (such as /bin/ls) in an absolute path or a relative path, and if so, execute it directly.

Step 2: Linux system checks whether the command entered by the user is an "alias command", i.e. replaces the original command name with a custom command name. You can use the alias command to create a command alias of your own in the format "alias = command".

To cancel a command alias, use the unalias command in the format "unalias alias." When we used the rm command to delete files before, the Linux system would ask us to confirm whether or not to delete the files. In fact, this is the rm alias command specially set by the Linux system to prevent users from deleting files by mistake.

Step 3: Bash interpreter judges whether the user inputs an internal command or an external command. Internal commands are instructions inside the interpreter and will be executed directly. However, the user inputs external commands most of the time, and these commands are handed over to step 4 for further processing. "type Command Name" can be used to determine whether the command entered by the user is an internal command or an external command.

Step 4 The system searches for the command file entered by the user in multiple PATHs, and the variable defining these paths is called path, which can be simply understood as "the interpreter's little assistant".

Its function is to tell the Bash interpreter where the command to be executed may be stored, and the Bash interpreter will obediently search in these locations one by one. PATH is a variable composed of multiple path values, each separated by a colon. The addition and deletion of these paths will affect the Bash interpreter's search for Linux commands.

Here is a more classic question: "why can't you add the current directory (.) to PATH?"

The reason is that although the current directory (.) can be added to the PATH variable, in some cases the user can avoid the trouble of entering the path where the command is located. However, if the hacker stores a Trojan file with the same name as ls or cd commands in the common public directory /tmp, and the user happens to execute these commands in the public directory, it is very likely that he will be caught.

Therefore, as cautious and experienced operation and maintenance personnel, after taking over a Linux system, they will certainly check whether there is any suspicious directory in the PATH variable before executing the command.

In addition, readers will also feel that the environment variable is particularly useful from the previous PATH variable example. We can use env command to view all the environment variables in the Linux system.

Linux, as a multi-user and multi-task operating system, can provide each user with an independent and appropriate working environment. Therefore, the same variable will have different values due to different user identities. For example, we use the following command to see what values the HOME variable has under different user identities.

In fact, variables are made up of fixed variable names and variable values set by users or the system. We can completely create variables ourselves to meet work requirements.

In the next section we will discuss about advanced shell concepts. Follow along!

Advanced Shell Concepts

The shell terminal interpreter can be regarded as a "translator" between human and computer hardware. It is used as a communication medium between users and the Linux system. In addition to supporting various variables and parameters, a shell terminal interpreter also provides control structure characteristics unique to high-level programming languages such as loops and branches. To correctly use these features in the Shell, it is particularly important to issue commands accurately.

Shell script commands work in two ways: interactive and batch.

Interactive: The user executes each command immediately.

Batch: The user writes a complete Shell script in advance, and the Shell will execute many commands in the script at one time.

Many Linux commands, regular expressions, pipe symbols, data stream redirection and other syntax rules learned before will be used in Shell scripts, and internal functions need to be modularized and processed through logical statements to finally form Shell scripts seen in daily life.

Looking at the SHELL variables, you can see that the current system already uses Bash as the command line terminal interpreter by default:

[root@sample ~]# echo $SHELL

/bin/bash

It is estimated that readers will feel tired and unloved after reading the complicated description of Shell scripts in the above article. However, the above refers to the writing principle of an advanced Shell script. Using Vim editor to write Linux commands into a file in sequence, this is a simple script.

For example, if you want to view the current working path and list all files and attribute information in the current directory, the script to implement this function should look like this:

[root@sample ~]# vim srujan.sh

The name of the Shell script file can be arbitrary, but to avoid being mistaken for an ordinary file, it is recommended to add the. sh, suffix to indicate that it is a script file.

In the above example.sh script, there are three different elements: the script declaration (#!) is used to tell the

178

system which Shell interpreter to use to execute the script; The comment information (#) in the second line is the introduction information of the script function and some commands so that oneself or others can quickly know the function of the script or some warning information when they see the script content in the future. The executable statements on the third and fourth lines are the Linux commands that we usually execute.

In addition to directly running the Shell script file with the bash interpreter command above, the second way to run the script program is by entering the full path. However, by default, an error message will be prompted due to insufficient permissions. At this time, it is only necessary to add execution permissions to the script file.

However, script programs like the above can only perform some predefined functions, which is too rigid. For the Shell script program to better meet some real-time requirements of the user and to finish the work flexibly, the script program must receive the parameters input by the user as it did when executing the command.

179

The Shell scripting language in the Linux system has already considered these and has built-in variables for receiving parameters. Spaces can be used between variables. For example, $0 corresponds to the name of the current Shell script program, $ # corresponds to a total of several parameters, $ * corresponds to the parameter values of all locations, $? The corresponding is to display the return value of the last command execution, while $1, $2, $3 ... respectively corresponding to the parameter value of the nth position.

Although the most basic Shell scripts can be written at this time by using Linux commands, pipe characters, redirection, and conditional test statements, such scripts are not suitable for production environments. The reason is that it cannot adjust the specific execution command according to the real work demand, nor can it realize automatic circular execution according to certain conditions. For example, we need to create 1,000 users in batch. First, we need to judge whether these users already exist. If they do not exist, they are automatically and sequentially created by scripts through loop statements.

Automation by Advanced shell scripting

Experienced system operation and maintenance engineers can enable Linux to automatically enable or stop certain services or commands within a specified period without human intervention, thus realizing automation of operation and maintenance. Although we already have a powerful script program to execute some batch processing work, it would be too painful if you still need to hit the enter key at 2 a.m. every day to execute the script program.

Planning tasks are divided into one-time planning tasks and long-term planning tasks, which can be understood as follows.

One-time planning task: start the website service at 11: 30 tonight.

Long-term planning task: pack and backup the/home/linux directory to takeback.tar.gz at 3: 25 a.m. every Monday.

As the name implies, a one-time scheduled task is executed only once and is generally used to meet temporary work requirements. We can use at command to realize this function, just write "at Time". If you want to view one-time scheduled tasks that have been set up but not yet executed, you can use the "at -l" command.

To delete it, you can use "atrm Task Sequence Number". When using at command to set up one-time scheduled tasks, interactive method is adopted by default. For example, use the following command to set the system to automatically restart the website service at 23:30 tonight.

[root@sample ~]# at 11:23

at > systemctl restart {enter parameter}

[root@sample ~]# at -l

2 Fri May 12 11:23:00 2019 Root

If the reader wants to challenge the more difficult but more simple way, he can put the pipe character (arbitrary gate) learned earlier between the two commands, and let the at command receive the output information of the previous echo command, so as to achieve the goal of creating a planned one-time task in a non-interactive way.

[root@sample ~]# echo "controloption restart service" | at 11:23

2 Fri May 12 11:23:00 2019 Root

[root@sample ~]# at -l

2 Fri May 12 11:23:00 2019 Root

3 Fri May 12 11:23:00 2019 Root

If we accidentally set up two one-time scheduled tasks, we can easily delete one of them by using the following command:

[root@sample ~]# atrm 2

[root@sample ~]# at -l

If we want the Linux system to perform certain specific tasks periodically and regularly, the crond service enabled by default in the Linux system is simply perfect. The command to create and edit a scheduled task is "crontab -e", the command to view the current scheduled task is "crontab -l", and the command to delete a scheduled task is "crontab -r". In addition, if you are logged in as an administrator, you can also add the -u parameter to the crontab command to edit other people's scheduled tasks.

Before formally deploying the planned tasks, please read the pithy formula "the order of minutes, hours, days, months and weeks". This is the parameter format for setting tasks using the crond service. It should be noted that if some fields are not set, asterisks (*) placeholder.

Suppose that at 3: 25 a.m. every Monday, Wednesday and Friday, the tar command is required to package the data directory of a certain website as a backup file. We can use the crontab -e command to create scheduled tasks. You do not need to use the -u parameter to create a scheduled task for yourself, and the specific parameters to realize the effect are shown in the results of crontab -l command:

[root@sample ~]# crontab -e

[root@sample ~]# crontab -l

It should be noted that in addition to using commas (,) to represent multiple time periods respectively, for example, "8,9,12" means August, September and December. A minus sign (-) can also be used to indicate a continuous period of time (for example, if the value of the field "day" is "12-15", it means the 12th to 15th of each month). And the interval between tasks is indicated by a division (/) (e.g., "*/2" indicates that tasks are executed every 2 minutes).

If you need to include multiple command statements for scheduled tasks at the same time in the crond service, write only one command statement per line. For example, we add another scheduled task whose function is to automatically empty all files in the /tmp directory from Monday to Friday at 1 a.m.

It is especially important to note that in the scheduled task parameters of the crond service, all commands must be written in absolute path. if you do not know the absolute path, please use the whereis command to query. the rm command path is the bolded part of the output information below.

[root@sample ~]# whereis rm

With this we have completed a brief introduction to Advanced shell programming. In the next chapter we will discuss about Log analysis and File transfer in detail. Follow Along!

Chapter 12: Log Management in Linux

Logs are created for analysis or to troubleshoot over an issue. Whenever an attack happens or if you are willing to go through your past actions the most logical thing to perform is to investigate a log file. Almost every operating system offers log files for their users better understanding. Being an operating system that is significantly used by technical users Linux offers a lot more abilities and options in log analysis when compared with normal day-to-day life operating systems such as Windows and Mac.

Usually, administrators and users only learn about log files when there is a sudden mishap or crisis in the system. However, if you want a sudden and fast reflex solution for a problem it is better to be thorough with the log analysis. This chapter will give you a brief and thorough introduction to Log analysis in Linux using various commands.

What are the Logs?

Logs are continuous storage of timeline events of every application that is involved in the Linux system. Linux logging system automatically stores them in the system for troubleshooting purposes.

It should be remembered that Linux applications can create log files on their specified directory. For example, Google chrome Linux browser uses a chrome directory to store the logs. Linux system specifications allow applications to keep logs on their desired location.

Every Linux system delivers logs and stores them in /var/log directory. Remember that only root users can edit or read the log files present. Linux makes log files for every system. Kernel system, package managers, booting procedure, database resources, and every other system procedure produces logs.

Log files store all the errors that systems deal with and can be an easy catch for attackers to understand all the activities that the root user and other users perform. Log files are like a weapon on your hands which can be used for both good and bad purposes.

Forensic investigators usually use a logging system to find about the whereabouts of any attacks that exploited the system. However, hackers are often intelligent and often manipulate or change the log files into an unreadable format.

In the next section, we will discuss log analysis in detail. Follow along!

Why the Log analysis is important?

There are numerous incidents that destroyed whole company's reputation and destroyed the resources. Worm attacks and viruses often occur in a cumulative time and can be stopped if given a chance to analyze the logs that are going on in the system.

Multinational Companies usually make their logging systems while using Linux whereas few of them buy already premade logging systems. As a matter of fact

Linux provides some great third party tools that can complete the log analysis with best results.

Linux log analysis

Log files often consists of a lot of valuable information but they are often very difficult to extract due to their complex format. However, there are a lot of tools that can make Linux users process easier. The most famous utility technique is Grep to find the Log files.

A lot of companies have developed advanced analytic tools to analyze the log files now days. These services provide log summaries and charts after a careful analysis of all your log files.

In this section we Will explain some of the most common methods to perform log analysis

1) grep

Grep is a search tool and is even available in windows to search the log files. Grep follows the basic model and searches the plain text with utmost perfection. Grep uses various parameters ro search the files. Here we will explain an example for your better understanding

To utilize grep in a perfect way you need to know what you are searching for. It is not an automatic process to find the results without any clue. So, make a brainstorm and write down the search string that will give you valid results.

For example, " user sample" string indicates that user named sample has accessed the system. So, to Check the log file on this parameter enter the following command and wait for the results

grep " user sample" /var/log/Auth.log

Output will give results with the line of the search string. You can further analyze it's time by using various parameters. Grep is one of the Most important tools that Linux administrators should be aware of.

The next log analysis technique is to use regular expressions

2 Regular Expressions

Regular expressions are traditionally used to remove the unnecessary waste in the results. Regular expressions help us to obtain exact results.

Example:

For example, imagine that there is an open port attack on "6324" and someone has got access. We need to find the authentication time using the port number.

When we try to search using the exact number we will get a lot of results that are coincided with the timestamp, URL or some other string entities that are present in the log. To not get these results in the search we can use regular expressions as shown below

grep -P (?<=port\s) 6324" /var/log/Auth.log

Another famous technique to perform log analysis is by performing the Surround search method.

Surround search is a technique to get the log lines before and after the successful search. An example can help you understand the advantage of Surround search.

For example, your server is receiving huge anonymous requests more than the normal load. You thought of Surround searching technique to analyze whether there is an ongoing brute force attack or not. In the next section we will discuss about syslog files in detail along with examples.

Syslog

Syslog is a general logging functionality that Linux distros provide from its users. It is an automatic service which receives logging requests from the applications and send them back to a server or address according to the user requirements.

How syslog works?

Syslog is a host configured tool that activates a logging system in the whole Linux system. When syslog starts works a lot goes around the back. We will try to explain this in detail for your better understanding about the Logging system in Linux. Follow along!

1) First of all, syslog searches for an entry to make it start using the service. This entry is located in the directory " \etc\syslog". After a successful start of the service syslog can be executed.

2) And after the start of the service syslogd monitors every application that is running in the Linux and constantly monitors the log files and monitors them with the syslog configuration file.

3) If any similarities are found for the Application log files and the Configuration file of syslogd then that particular log message will be stored as a seperate log files or by given instructions of the user.

This is the exact procedure how syslog works. In the next section we will discuss in detail about the syslog entry analysis.

Sys log entry analysis

These are usually four analysis factors that can be used to determine the logging functionality. They are very important for understanding the log details.

1) Facility

2) Priority

3) Selector

4) Action

In this section we will have a brief discussion about all the four concepts so that you can get a good understanding about the Log entry analysis.

1) Facility

This entity stores the information about the file or application that has sent the log report. There are a lot of application availabilities such as File transfer protocol, Mail etc.

Here we will discuss about some of the most important syslog facilities.

a) auth

When you find this in the log file then remember that it represents sensitive information of authorization. Some of the examples include login,getty.

b) cron

Cron is an automatic scheduler functionality available in the Linux system. All the log messages that are delivered by the scheduler can be found with this facility.

c) Kern

Kernel as we all know is the most important entity that runs the Linux system. Usually kernel sends different messages to the other systems. This facility can help us dig information about the kernel.

d) Mail

Mail protocol is very essential as a lot of communication is now resided on it. Using this facility, you can look at the logging information of your messages, recipients and a lot other.

e) Ftp

File transfer protocol is a service that Linux offers to transfer files in a remote computer. A lot of information is logged during this procedure which can be easily acquired using this facility.

There are a lot of other facilities which can be used for better Log analysis.

2) Priority

Priority is one of the important parameters present in the logging system. It makes sense to look at log files that need to be dealt in a quick way. You can easily filter log files based on priority. Here are some important priority factors that need to be known.

a) emerg

This is used when there is an extremely critical condition in the system

b) Alert

Alert makes us remember the catastrophe that the system is going to face. Continuous log analysis is a must to look back at alerts and deal with them.

c) err

This is another parameter that needs to be looked at as soon as possible. Errors can make system functionalities halt.

Selector and Action

With the above-mentioned parameters, we can easily filter out the valid and required logs. Now with these filters there are often a lot of Logs that will be tracked. However, it is not reliable to look at every log that is present. So, we use selector and Action functionalities to further filter the only Log files we are looking for.

For example: By using the selector and action we can only filter Emergency log files that deals with system.

We need to know about Message selector and Message action before continuing to the next section.

a) Message selector

Message selector is the functionality that checks which logs are important and necessary from a bundle of Log files that are available.

b) Message Action

Message action is a parameter that makes us to say what we can do with the selected Message. You can program in a way such that they can be sent to a server or a text file.

A lot of companies like Loggy are developing software's to make this easy by making everything automatic according to your requirements. You can research about Third party Logging solutions if you are interested.

Logging Actions and Logger Command

Here are the famous Logging Actions that needs to be learned a Linux administrator for better organization of the resources.

a) Send all the logged messages to a user or to a pre-defined server. This is usually done automatically. All you need to do is enter the information before.

b) You can send all the selected log messages to all users and also to specific users. Remember to use an asterisk when you are trying to send to all users.

c) You can also send the selected log messages to syslog that is activated in your network or remote network. This will become handy when you are working with a team.

Logger command is a special utility that Linux offers for its users for better Log analysis. You can enter parameters such as priority easily to get valid information. In the next section we will discuss about Log Rotation in detail and end this chapter.

Log Rotation

Log files usually are of less size. However, as time passes Linux systems generate Log files in abundant size. Log files can quickly fill up your space and cause system inefficiency. For this reason, it is recommended to use the Log rotation facility available in Linux systems to automatically send your log files according to a pre-defined quality.

As we discussed before this is automatic and controlled by crondameon of the Linux system. Logrotate utility can also compress the log files for decreasing the size.

Using logrotate is a complex task and requires you to create a separate configuration file for better results. In this section we will explain a brief procedure to make Log rotation work for your system. Follow along!

1) Start an example Configuration file

First look at the logrotate.conf file and give root permission to it. You can change the rotate change time such as weekly or monthly in the configuration file.

Use and fill parameters such as rotate, compress to substantially increase the impact of the log rotation mechanism.

2) Add that configuration file to the system log

Now you need to send this log rotation configuration file to /etc/logrotate.d for linking it.

3) Customize

In this step you can customize various options such as log rotate, shared scripts to increase the efficiency of the system.

After customizing all you need to do is start running using the following command:

root@sample : logrotate /etc/logrotate.conf --debug

With this we have completed this book. We have discussed a lot of examples and concepts in detail in this chapter. Hope you had a good ride by reading this book.

Conclusion

Glad that you have completed this book. Hope you have learnt a lot of valuable information from this book. We have discussed in detail about various Linux commands and Linux features with precise information.

What to do now?

After reading this book it is better if you can use these commands present to experiment in your Linux system. Look at Linux forums and blogs to further enhance your skills.

Linux is an operating system that is available in different forms. Experience can help you fall in Love with Linux. Try different Linux distros and experiment with different Linux tools.

Make yourself well abundant by reading various Linux books and blogs. If you ever face any errors try to know about them by researching in Google. GitHub repositories can also be a vast knowledge.

Hope you have learnt a lot of knowledge from this book. Wishing you all the best!